W9-CAV-546

BE MY GUEST

THEME PARTY SAVOIR-FAIRE

Happy Birthday Rachel!
May there always
be reason to party.

♥ Rosie

(Will see you at The Mill.)

601 West 26th Street, 18th Floor
New York, NY 10001, USA
Tel: 212-989-6769 Fax: 212 647-0005
www.assouline.com

ISBN: 2 84323 345 3

10 9 8 7 6 5 4 3 2

Color separation: Gravor, Switzerland.

Printed in China

Copyedited by Jennifer Ditsler

RENA KIRDAR SINDI

PHOTOGRAPHS BY JESSICA CRAIG-MARTIN

BE MY GUEST

THEME PARTY SAVOIR-FAIRE

ASSOULINE

Contents

Preface

I wish I could say that I've been to more than a few thrilling, over-the-top costume parties over the years. There simply aren't enough of them anymore, and when they do happen—when that teasing invite arrives, a treasure map, perhaps, scrolled inside a bottle, or a slip of Mylar that instantly evokes the glamour of a seventies disco—it's not always easy to rally the troops into their borrowed finery for the occasion.

Maybe we live in too minimal a time. Maybe we're too busy, too tired, too self-conscious for the kind of fantasy that Marie-Hélène de Rothschild so eloquently proposed at her Surrealist Dinner and that Truman Capote offered up at his legendary Black and White Ball. But I don't think so, and I don't think anyone who's been to any of my theme parties—be it a dinner at home slapped together last-minute or a big New York benefit at Cipriani—would say so either.

I'll never forget that first excited shock that hit me when I walked into Pia and Christopher Getty's "Tarzan and Jane" party many summers ago. It was a warm July night in Southampton, Long Island, and the torch-lit tent on the Gettys's lawn reverberated with the rhythms of African drums.

Everywhere I looked, the buttoned-up women I knew from the city floated by in tiny, cut-suede dresses, loosely knotted sarongs, coconut bras and leopard spots. Their husbands had traded in their suits for loincloths, cheetah-print G-strings and, in my own husband's case, Zulu warrior garb in the form of a shield and not much else. He dragged me into the tent on a rope, which stunned more than a few guests but earned us Pia's prize for best costume: a sterling silver banana, fancifully engraved with the date of the party.

It may seem silly to say, but that banana is precisely what this book is about. An unforgettable party can be distilled down to the most unlikely detail—and whether that's a quirky and hilarious invitation, a fabulous table setting, an incredible cake (Pia's was seven feet long and shaped like a banana) or a great deejay, I'd like to show you how to make your parties unforgettable, too.

The fourteen theme parties in this book can be adapted to two, two hundred or two thousand people, for the celebration of a special occasion or, better still, for no occasion at all. For me, a theme is an occasion in and of itself; time and again, it's offered me the rare and welcome opportunity to be someone else for a night. What follows are the great escapes that have worked for me, and with the practical advice this book offers—where to shop, whom to call, how to set it all up—I think they'll work for you as well.

I should add that, while the adults in my life love to get into costume and into character, so especially do the children—and most if not all the themes proposed in this book would delight a child. Some of them already have: When my daughter, Leana, was five, she was already something of a party expert, and had planned a themed event for each birthday from age six to fifteen. Of course, I had dibs on her sixteenth.

Introduction

Why is it that there are so few great parties anymore? Maybe it's a question that plagues every generation of partygoer, but I really do believe that my peer group is a little lost when it comes to having fun. It's easy to throw a proper party, with beautiful food, flattering light and a well-balanced list of guests, but it's much harder to throw an unforgettable event—a magical night on which, somehow, everything works and everyone glitters, the kind of party you remember for years and count yourself lucky to have attended.

I love that kind of party, and quite frankly, I miss it. As a New Yorker, I go to dozens of black-tie affairs every year, which begin to take on the drab, impersonal character of lavish business dinners. The parties in this book are designed to free us from the feeling of a party as business—these are parties to delight us, not impress us, to transport, not transfix.

Planning a Party

Some of the best parties are thrown for no reason more than to celebrate good friendship and good fun. Setting the party date is a crucial, and sometimes tricky, early step in the process. There are reasons for celebrating in every season, but a good rule of thumb is to avoid those times when you and your friends are thoroughly partied out (in the first week of January, for example) or hopping in and out of town (during the month of August, say). Whether you choose a weekday or a weekend depends on your lifestyle; many city dwellers spend the weekends in the country and may be irked to surrender their days away. What's more, many may find themselves so tired by the time the weekend comes that what they'd really like to do on a Friday night is relax at home and spend time with their family.

The Type of Party

What should you throw? A luncheon, a tea, a cocktail, a dinner or a dance? Lunches, teas and weekend brunches are the obvious choice for a ladies' event—a baby or bridal shower, a girls' birthday party—and for children's parties. Cocktails might make sense for a large and not very cohesive group, but they're not my favorite way to entertain. I dispute the idea that a cocktail party is the simplest option. A well-orchestrated cocktail party can end up costing almost as much as a dinner, and in the end, you get much less "value" for your money. At events where people wander in an out over a two- or three-hour time period, conversation rarely presses past the superficial, and the sense of an end point gives people much less incentive to relax.

Dinner parties are my favorite way to entertain, and, I believe, most people's favorite way to be entertained. Although there are a few buffets in this book, I prefer a seated dinner: Fewer dishes are required—there's never a need for more than three courses—and the seating impels your guests to get to know one another, which is the greatest pleasure that any party has to offer.

The Seating

You may choose free seating or allocated seating, but my preference for parties of more than ten is the latter. Only when the party is small and tight-knit is free seating a happy option; otherwise, people enjoy having seating assigned for them as it relieves all those old and die-hard anxieties from the school lunchroom! Allocated seating is more time-consuming and expensive, on account of the need for place cards and escort cards, but if the time is carefully invested, the rewards can be huge. Creative seating does require thought. What strands of commonality can you find between two guests that they too might discover and enjoy over the course of an evening? What business relationships or, better still, romantic possibilities can you encourage? Just be sure to deploy diplomacy, caution, sensitivity and mischief in equal measure—and if you haven't the time for them, then don't bother with allocated seating. No matter what, there will always be a person (or a few people) who thinks he deserved a "better" seat. But if he wishes to be invited back, he'll never tell you that.

Seating, like love, is a subject on which it's nearly impossible to advise. But here are a few tips culled from all those long nights I've spent in my den arranging and rearranging tables, very often with my friend Serena Boardman, a virtuosa of *placement*, at my side.

1) Don't put all the "fun" people at the same table.
2) Don't seat couples beside one another. Unless they're very timid, put them at different tables so that, after dinner, each person has a natural destination in the other person. This ensures circulation, and it gives a couple two sets of experiences to share when they get home.
3) Do what I do: Invest in a binder stocked with clear plastic leaflets. In each leaflet, put a piece of paper on which you've drawn or printed pictures of your tables. Then use little round stickers in two colors (one for women, the other for men) with your guests' names on them, which you can move around on the plastic to play with different seating possibilities from table to table.
4) Don't do the seating until the day before, as you'll always get last-minute cancellations.
5) Be aware of any major problems between your guests, and avoid the temptation to play peacemaker through seating. Keep these people well apart.
6) Whisper that thing you think might link two guests. It would be a shame for them to spend an entire dinner without realizing their shared interest in, say, disco music or 17th-century English furniture.

The Theme

Don't make the mistake of thinking that only costume parties require themes. All parties do, even if it's only the color of the linens or the variety of the foods, to bring cohesion to the room. The great thing about a theme party is its consistency—the way the invitation, the décor, the menu, the music and the dress code all communicate the same message. But lavish theme parties like those in this book require plenty of time to plan. Give yourself at least two months, and your guests at least three weeks, since so much of what makes a theme party great lies in the preparations.

Holiday parties often have built-in themes, but it's nice to vary those a little so that the parties defy expectation. For a Valentine's Day party, I focused on legendary lovers—encouraging my guests to come as Antony and Cleopatra, Napoleon and Josephine, Elvis and Priscilla—and chose purple instead of red as the thematic color. (It's just as romantic.)

In choosing the theme, it's also important to consider whom you'll be inviting. Remember that you need the full participation and excitement of your guests to make a successful event. You don't want to overwhelm them; if the costumes seem impossibly difficult, even your most stalwart friends may make no effort at all. Try to find something that's novel without being intimidating.

The List

As a rule, invite 20 percent more people than you actually want to allow for regrets and cancellations. (And remember that more men cancel.) Try to resist the temptation to say, "If I'm having so-and-so then I must have so-and-so." Give yourself the guest list you really want. Diversity is essential to any party, and I like to mix generations and personality types, to repay people for their invitations and to initiate new friendships.

The Venue

There are three places you can have a party: at home, at a restaurant or in a raw rented space. In a city like New York, especially, where so much social life takes place in public, an invitation to someone's home is especially welcome. But unless you're like Muriel Brandolini, the décor of whose townhouse was a perfect match for her Vietnamese dinner, mounting a theme party at home isn't easy. Remember, though, that you can do a fabulous dinner for ten, totally in theme, simply by decorating your dining room table.

If you can find a restaurant whose size, décor and menu fits your theme, then you're a very lucky party thrower indeed. But the shape of the restaurant is a key ingredient to the party. One room is optimal; multiple spaces tend to divide and defuse a party. Cocktails in one room and dinner in another works, but dinner in two rooms generally doesn't. If a party is to include dancing, it's a big mistake to set the dance floor off in a different room; dancing should be part of a party's natural evolution.

A raw space is perfect if you have the budget and the time to dedicate to building a theme party from the ground up. It should be big enough to accommodate all your guests, but not so big that it ever looks sparse. (There is nothing more deadly to a party than empty space—it should be warm and chock-full, but not crushed.) But you'll be responsible for everything, or at least for delegating everything, from the décor and the menu and the waitstaff to the tables, chairs, flatware and glasses. This book's glossary offers a list of the New York caterers, decorators, florists, costumers and rental agencies that I used for these parties.

The Menu

Where party food is concerned, you have three options: home-cooked, cooked at a restaurant or catered. The wonderful thing about homemade food is that, whatever it is (and that includes mediocre!), it's always appreciated. But if you don't love to cook, don't cook. If you do love to cook, however, keep this cardinal rule in mind: Do as much as you possibly can in advance. There is nothing worse than a party where the hostess spends much of the evening slaving away in her kitchen. Forget the cliché that insists it's impossible to enjoy one's own party—it just isn't true.

When you throw a party at a restaurant, it's easiest to choose a place whose menu is a natural companion to your theme. Composing set menus is the best way to control the cost, though it's smart to offer two or even three options for the main course.

Nothing is more delightful than dishes that wittily capture the given theme. (A friend of mine once threw a "blue dinner," where he served beautiful homemade blue beet-and-ricotta ravioli, halibut in a blue cream sauce over blue mashed potatoes, and chocolate cake with blue icing.)

If you're using a caterer, try to sample his or her food before the night of the party. More than restaurants, caterers will be especially open to incorporating your ideas—both for the food and for the thematic embellishments. If you're throwing the party at home or in a rented space, caterers will also provide their own serving utensils, and they usually know just where to rent tableware if you need it.

It's always fun to concoct a signature drink for your theme—a margarita for a Mexican fiesta, for example, or a tropical island punch for a luau. Presenting row upon row of the same drink on a giant silver tray (or on a wooden block, a plate of glass, or an upended mirror) is both attractive and easy. Having one thematic drink means the bartender doesn't have to worry about juggling a table full of bottles and a crowd full of whims. Remember that guests at a party often like to be passive. Drinking what we're told to drink can, in its way, be very liberating!

The Invitation

It's easy to underestimate the seductive powers of the perfect invitation. But there's no better or more effective way to set the tone of the party than on that simple slip of paper. Where theme parties are concerned, the invitation itself is an important motivating factor: Even your most enthusiastic friends need to be excited into full participation in the theme, and an invitation that richly captures that theme will encourage your friends to do the same. In my opinion, the invitation is absolutely not the place to skimp on either time or money; it's here that you can inspire your guests and tease them with a little of the magic that your party promises.

An inspiring invitation is not necessarily an expensive invitation. Vivid color and offbeat shapes, for example, are easy ways both to capture the theme and to help the invitation jump out in a mundane pile of bills. The invitation must seize on the theme in a way that will encourage your friends, so you need to pinpoint the dominant symbols of that theme before you set about crafting it.

The simplest route is a paper invitation sent by mail. These you can order or make yourself with paper, stencils, stickers and colorful pens from the local stationer. I'm a fan of paper invitations that include a pasted-in photograph of the hosts or guest of honor in the costume of the theme; for example, a great idea for a punk party might be to dress up in advance, take a picture, and convert it into a punk postcard of the type sold all over London. As with any theme, pinpointing the most evocative symbols—whether they're studded collars and Mohawks or stars and stripes—is the key to a successful invitation.

If you have the budget, an elaborate invitation—in three dimensions—is the best way to kick up your friends' spirits. For her luau, Marjorie Gubelmann sent out Barbie-size hula dolls that danced to their own music with invitations tied to their necks. Part of the budget for this type of invitation must be allotted to shipping—but all told, the impact is great. As you'll see, these are the invitations I love to make.

A few words of wisdom: If you need to invite people at the last minute because the numbers are too low, make sure you seat those people very well; otherwise, they'll feel like fillers. For a party beginning at 8 or 9 pm, make it very clear whether dinner will be served. And always be clear when you're expecting costumes, since the best theme parties are those for which every guest makes an equal effort. Strange though it may seem, the more you leave for interpretation, the less likely people will be to dress up.

The Entertainment

There is really only one question when it comes to choosing music for a party: To dance or not to dance? For a party with dancing, the trick is to start slowly and work you way up both in volume and in rhythm. A good general rule is to start the hip-shaking music towards the end of the main course, but an even better general rule is to try to feel the mood of your guests and adapt to it. A good deejay will be able to do this, too.

Where hired entertainment is concerned, I prefer a deejay to a cover band. A deejay is more apt—with your guidance—to play what people want to hear. He also comes cheaper! A terrific mariachi band or African drumming trio or any other exceptional specialty outfit is fun too.

Either make your deejay a list in advance or discuss with him exactly what kind of music you want and when you want it. If your party has an exotic theme, start with the appropriate music (let it pipe over the crowd as they arrive, and if it's mellow enough, let it set the mood at dinner), then have it gradually give way to the familiar songs your friends like to dance to. Stick to the same guidelines if you're doing your own deejaying: If you can, burn a few CDs beforehand and label them "cocktails," "background" and "dancing."

It can be a treat to supplement the music with other, more surprising entertainments. I hired belly dancers for my "1001 Nights" party and a handwriting specialist for my "Signature Styles" dinner. Other ideas to consider: magicians, fortune tellers, pianists and clowns. Believe me—in the right doses, adults enjoy these too.

The Décor, Lighting and Atmosphere

If you're entertaining at home, choose an area of your house or apartment that is compatible with, or easily adapted to, the theme. Concentrate on a beautiful thematic table whose cloth, settings, place cards, centerpiece and embellishments all point to the same grand idea: My feeling is that the more decorative whimsy you pile on, the better the effect. Centerpieces are the perfect means to offer up a novel interpretation of a less than novel theme; flowers, on top of being expensive, can be boring by comparison.

For evening affairs, keep your lighting dim: lots of candles and very little, if anything, else. If you're a person who tends to err on the bright side, reconsider. If you're entertaining at a restaurant, make sure you've seen to the lighting in advance; it can provide an unfortunate surprise otherwise. For parties in which you're dealing with multiple dining tables, escort cards are a good idea. Like invitations, these are powerful vehicles for your theme, so choose the design carefully.

Keep in mind that most raw spaces need significant decorating to warm them up. Potted trees, for one thing, fill in space and provide warmth. So do fabrics—suspended, slung and laid across tables. I like to decorate the tables with objects that my guests can use to enhance their costumes; feathers, for example, are a terrific alternative to flowers because they give height, warmth and lushness to a table, they look fabulous and cost little, and at the right theme party, women can pluck them from the vases and put them in their hair.

The Dress

Remember that at any theme party, your guests are the most powerful component of the décor and the best expression of the theme. It's the people, done up and decked out, who make a theme party take off and who provide its most memorable visual impressions. On top of sending a motivating invitation, you need to do your bit by spreading the word. People are, by nature, as terrified to dress in costume as they are thrilled to do it, so you need to assuage the terror and kindle the thrill in any way you can.

I prefer themes whose costumes are easy to create at home, either out of one's own closet or with a few supplementary items. Costume shops and rental agencies can produce some amazing ensembles—but they're never as satisfying as the quirky, personal stuff people come up with on their own. You should encourage your guests to take advantage of one of those rare moments in which they're permitted to be someone else.

The Photographs

I very much regret those times when I failed to have photographs of my own parties. The event comes and goes, and it's nice to have something to jog the memory. Leave disposable cameras lying around (and beg your friends not to take them home), or, for special occasions, hire a professional. It's wonderful to be able to send your guests a few select prints afterwards.

One Final Note: Don't worry. Once I walk into my own party, the obsessing is finished. There is nothing more to be done, and it's time to relax and enjoy, and to give in to the inevitable arc of the night. Once I do, everyone else does the same. I'll never understand why people can't enjoy their own parties: It's the food and drink and décor you chose, the music you like to dance to, and the people you love. Of course, there will be hiccups. Seating may have to be tweaked at the last minute; you may have a no-show (who'd better call the following morning with a fantastic excuse). But that's all fine: Just take away

Hot Hacienda

I love the warmth and sensuality of Latin culture—its vivid hues, bubbling music and insatiable appetite for revelry that almost matches my own! A Mexican fiesta livens up a cold winter night and freshens a hot summer day, and it's a wonderfully versatile party—unintimidating but with ample room for sophistication—that adapts to a cozy dinner for ten just as well as a blowout for 400 or (minus the tequila) a child's birthday. The theme needn't confine itself to Mexico, either; it can focus on, or borrow from, the Spanish flamenco, Brazilian *carna al* and Argentine *asado* (those fantastic all-night barbecues).

A good way to begin planning your fiesta is to pinpoint the theme's richest symbols: sombreros, ponchos, shawls, piñatas, paper flowers, maracas, fans, cacti, tamales and mariachi bands. These lead naturally to the party's color scheme: rusty reds, burnt and bright oranges, faded and hot pinks.

Entertainment

When I threw a fiesta for 40 people in a boardroom at Christie's auction house in New York, I had the benefit of very good timing: The Latin American Art sale was around the corner, and we used scores of fabulous paintings by the likes of Diego Rivera to turn a drab corporate room into a cozily evocative little cave.

In 19th-century haciendas, walls were practically paved with pictures, and that's just what we tried to replicate by decorating densely. At the entrance, we erected an altar of amber votives and baskets of chili peppers, beans and Mexican candies—to which a vase of lilies and bunches of roses lent a little romance.

Papel cortado, Mexico's brightly colored tissue paper, hung on strings from the ceiling. Peasant-bloused waiters made guacamole on the spot and served it from giant lava stones, and from the moment they entered, nobody wanted for a margarita. At the dinner table, men's chairs bore sombreros and women's chairs were draped with Mexican silk shawls. We used an undercloth of bronze Dupione raw silk with an Aztec-motif runner down the middle, and let candlelight shine on red and orange chilis, tropical flowers and cacti.

Brown cotton napkins were tied with raffia; ladies' napkins were finished with a single yellow-lipped red rose, and men's napkins rested underneath an individual maraca. We used rustic, hand-blown Mexican barware and wood-handled flatware—all of which remained relatively intact until one guest, dressed in the Mexican Victorian style of a character out of *Dios de los Muertos*, capped the night by dancing on the table—something I always consider the sign of a great party.

Dress

Women should think ruffles, off-the-shoulder peasant tops, full gypsy skirts, sashes, mantillas in bright, mismatched colors, flowers in the hair, long, curly wigs, combs, silver jewelry and beads. Men might go for sombreros, ponchos, matador capes, Mariachi brocade and *rebozos* (colorful Spanish sashes), but a Mexican blanket and a moustache paired with a white shirt will do the trick. Waitstaff should keep to white shirts, hankies tied around the neck and sombreros.

Venue

Few of us live in fabulous Mexican-style houses, but any of us can transform a dining room or living room into a hacienda by creating a richly evocative table as the focal point of the evening. If you can, consider renting a room at a Mexican restaurant—the ideal one-stop-shop for food and atmosphere. Brick, stucco, low ceilings and rustic details make the ultimate locale, but you can personalize the restaurant yourself through the menu, décor and party favors, and relax while the waitstaff works out the logistics.

Invitations

The fiesta theme lends itself to rustic, home-made-looking cards that require only some imagination and the paper products available at your neighborhood stationer or party store. Choose a colorful card stock and mail it in an earthy envelope (I like the combination of bright orange and mustard). Decorate the card with stencils or stickers at the borders: a chili pepper, perhaps, or a tiny sombrero.

If you have more time, take a photograph of yourself and your co-hosts in full Mexican garb and glue it to the card; your guests, of course, will be inspired to do you one better when they arrive! If you're inviting a small group of guests who live close by, consider sending (by mail or messenger) tiny cacti with the invitations hanging from a tag. At a party store, you might find mini-sombreros you can write on directly, or mini-piñatas you can stuff at home with an invite. A paper flower delivered in a corsage box is a good idea, because guests like to receive something that can be used as part of the costume.

If you're feeling especially extravagant, send a poncho to each invitee—monogram it with his or her name if you like—or send a set of maracas with the invitation text painted directly onto them. In summer, I like to send a rustic box with all the fixings for a margarita to put my guests in the mood.

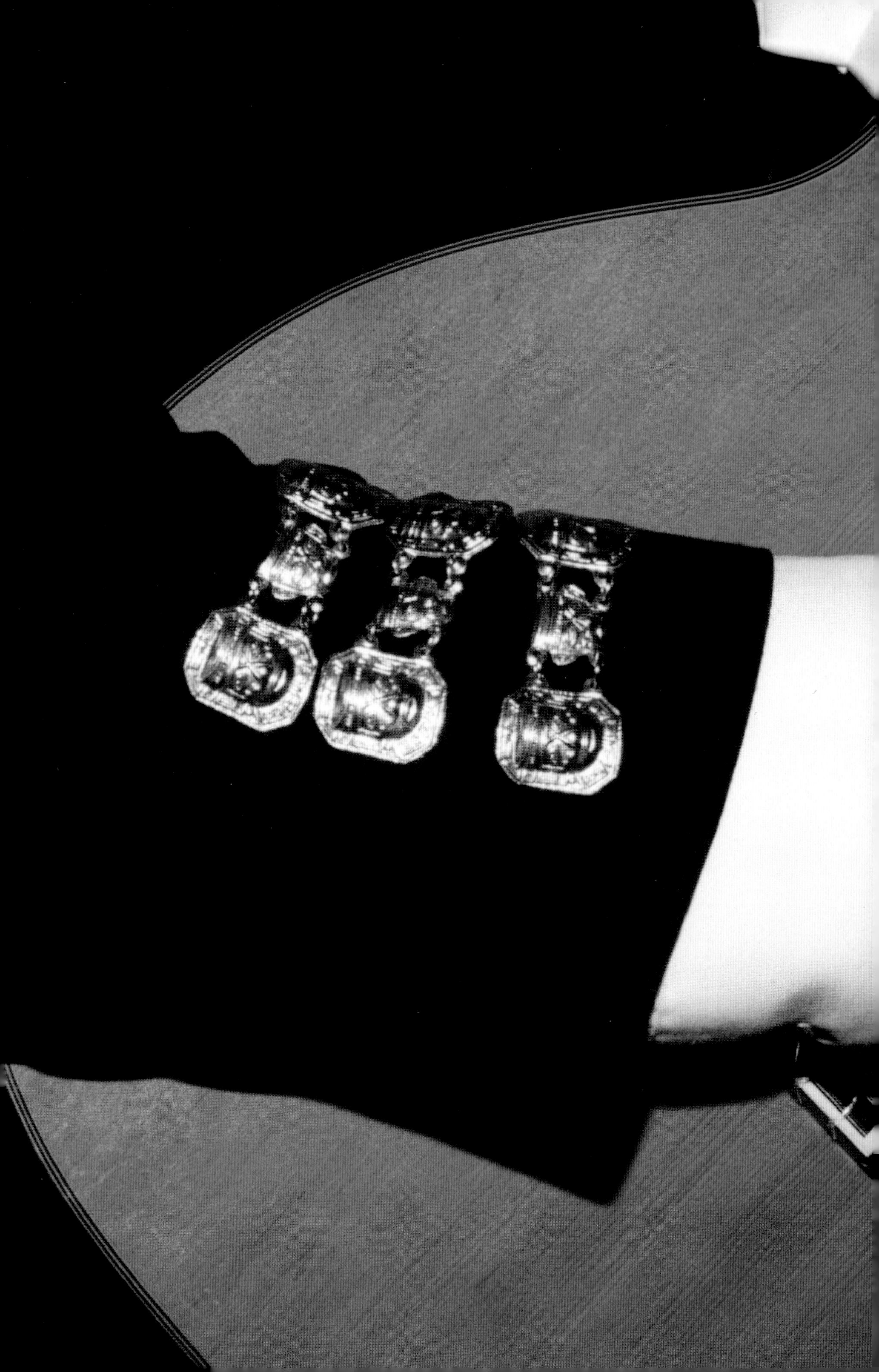

The focus here is fiesta: Spicy guacamole and tangy salsa with a cool, salty margarita and a sexy Latin beat set the mood for a night of dancing and revelry. Men in sombreros and women's bared shoulders lend a Mexican flavor to the sizzling festivities.

Menu

SERVES 4

MAIN COURSE

Huachinango (red snapper) Steamed in Banana Leaves with Yucateca Sauce

INGREDIENTS

YUCATECA SAUCE:

- 1 TBSP CORN OIL
- 8 TOMATILLOS, HUSKS REMOVED, CHOPPED ROUGHLY
- 2 JALAPENO PEPPERS, CHOPPED ROUGHLY WITH SEEDS
- 1 GREEN BELL PEPPER, SEEDS REMOVED, CHOPPED ROUGHLY
- 2 CLOVES GARLIC, CRUSHED
- 1/2 SMALL WHITE ONION, PEELED AND CHOPPED ROUGHLY
- 5 SCALLIONS, ROOT END REMOVED, CHOPPED ROUGHLY
- 1/4 BUNCH CILANTRO, LEAVES ONLY CHOPPED ROUGHLY
- 1/2 TSP CUMIN SEEDS
- 1/4 TSP MEXICAN DRY OREGANO
- 2 TBSP TOASTED MEXICAN PUMPKIN SEEDS (PEPITAS), GROUND
- JUICE OF 1 LIME
- JUICE OF 1/2 ORANGE
- SALT TO TASTE

PREPARATION

1) In a medium nonreactive sauce pan warm oil at low heat.
2) Add tomatillos, all peppers, garlic, onion, scallions, cilantro, cumin, oregano and pumpkin seeds.
3) Over medium-low heat, bring slowly to a simmer. Cover, cook 30 minutes, until tender.
4) Remove from heat, add juices, salt. Cool.

THE FISH

- 4 BANANA LEAVES, CUT INTO APPROX. 9-INCH SQUARES
- 1 GREEN PAPAYA, PEELED, SPLIT, SEEDED AND JULIENNED
- 2 TSP YUCATECA SAUCE
- 4 FILLETS OF RED SNAPPER, 6 OZ. EACH, SKIN REMOVED
- 1 JALAPENO PEPPER, SEEDED AND DICED
- SALT
- 1/4 BUNCH CILANTRO
- FRESH TAMALES

1) Lay out banana leaves shiny side down and place a small mound of papaya in the center of each. Layer each as follows: 1 teaspoon Yucateca sauce, fish, 1 teaspoon more Yucateca sauce, diced jalapeno, pinch of salt, cilantro sprig.
2) Fold the package into a rectangle by folding sides in, then ends under.
3) Prepare a steamer and steam fish package above active steam, covered, for approx. 15 minutes.
4) Open the package to check if the fish is done. It should be flaky and just cooked through.
5) Warm remaining Yucateca sauce.
6) When fish is ready, split top of package and pull apart to open, pour in 1 tablespoon of Yucateca sauce and serve with fresh tamales.

Cocktail

Pink Cadillac Margarita

3 oz Patron Gold
1 oz Cointreau
Splash Grand Marnier
Splash fresh lime juice

Combine ingredients, shake and pour over ice into a cocktail glass. Garnish with a lime wheel. (Salt optional.)

Music

•

Calle 54
Blue Note/Miramax
•

¡A Gozar!
Blue Note
•

Brazilian Classics (vols. 1 & 2)
Luaka Bop
•

The Girl From Ipanema
Astrud Gilberto/Polygram
•

Tito Puente and His Latin Jazz All-Stars
Concord Jazz
•

Brazil Now
Blue Note
•

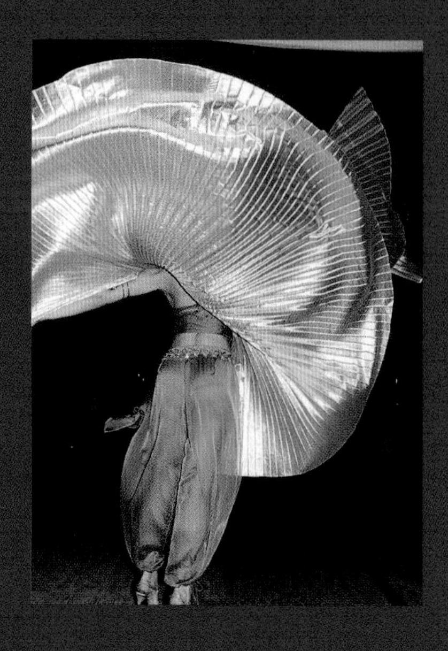

One Thousand & One Nights

For my husband's 30th birthday a few years ago, I planned a party that I'm afraid must have stunned more than a few of my New York friends. By carting in palm trees and Persian carpets, I transformed Mortimer's restaurant, that dearly departed temple of American restraint on Lexington Avenue, into a lavish Middle Eastern bazaar. It worked—not only because I made it work but because, as themes go, "1001 Nights" is wonderfully versatile. Screw red bulbs into your lamps and do it for ten friends at home, or take over a huge space—like the promenade of the State Theater, the scene of this benefit for the New York City Ballet—and invite 1001 people.

The medieval Arabian stories that makeup the *1001 Nights* are rich in party material, and it doesn't take much to evoke the mysterious majesty of palace pavilions with their charming recesses, secret chambers and mysterious passages. Remember, too, that your guests will forgive you (if they notice at all!) when you mix your metaphors a bit and add Moroccan, Egyptian and Indian embellishments to your magic carpet ride.

Dress

Invite your guests to dress for a magic carpet ride. Ladies might go as harem maids, gypsies or belly dancers—their veils lending the evening the quality of a masquerade ball—but even a stunning piece of jewelry or a sparkling headpiece can suffice to transform a simple dress. Men should wear djellabas and caftans, turbans and billowing Alladin pants.

Invitations

If you're sending out cards, keep in mind that deep, jewel-like colors best reflect this theme: rich reds, pinks, purples and blues, always set against gold. Using a gold marker, do your best to write out invitations in an Arabic-looking hand—full of undulating and curling letters. Attach a tassel to the envelope or stuff it with a Moroccan paper lantern or a silken veil instead of card stock, and throw in a few plastic jewels in place of confetti.

At the flea market or even at a Middle Eastern carpet store, you may be able to find a beat-up old rug, or scraps from one, out of which you can cut individual, invitation-size flying carpets. To the back of each scrap, glue a card that includes the party details—or roll a piece of parchment inside the carpet, tie it with a thick tassel and send it as a scroll. For a more elaborate and more humorous invitation, prepare miniature stuffed camels bearing tags, or a miniature tagged palm tree wrapped in colored cellophane for hand delivery. And if that doesn't quite cut it, consider sending a human telegram in the form of a belly dancer; in my experience, this doesn't go over well—or perhaps it simply goes over too well—at the office!

Venue

It's no joke that changing the color of your lightbulbs is the cheapest, easiest and often the most effective way of transforming the atmosphere of your home—in this case into a harem tent at dusk, with red, purple, pink and blue light alongside flickering candles. If you're not throwing this party at home, consider a Moroccan or Indian restaurant, keeping in mind that color should be among the primary criteria for selecting one. This is a terrific summer theme that loves a tent outdoors, but it's no more difficult to create a tented atmosphere inside by hanging inexpensive, colorful fabric against the walls.

Décor

"1001 Nights" is a theme that demands as many palm trees and peacock feathers (though some say they're bad luck), fans, lanterns, cushions and hookahs—decorative or not—as you can possibly cobble together. The important thing is to saturate the environment of this party, starting with deep, rich lighting, incense and pools of rose water. Pile oriental and kilim carpets onto the floor, and scatter them with giant cushions and flower petals.

For the New York City Ballet party, we laid the tables with *moukesh*, the richly patterned Indian fabric that is literally stamped with gold, and used Moroccan lamps and gilded palm trees as centerpieces. But you can achieve a lush, Middle Eastern effect with nothing more than red or purple cotton cloths, bowls of dates and olives and inexpensive glass plates that look like molten rubies.

The most important thing is to make each table look like a treasure chest laid open: I like to litter mine with multicolored votives, tassels and Egyptian worry beads. *Mezze*—the Middle Eastern equivalent of tapas—make wonderful hors d'œuvres for this theme: hummus and baba ghanoush, stuffed grape leaves, spinach pies and *kibbeh* (Lebanese meatballs). Serving food family-style works especially well here: Think curries, couscous and kabobs of all sorts.

Entertainment

For the cocktail hour, imagine the effect of a roomful of roaming fortune-tellers, belly dancers and mock concubines wielding peacock-feather fans. I'm never much of a fan of a dinner show, but I've seen guests go wild for a mid-course belly dance. An Arabian singer or band makes good sense during cocktails and for a bit of dancing, but I suggest you switch midway to more popular dance music—have the deejay pepper his set with a few Middle Eastern dance hits—if you want to keep your guests on the floor. In a tented nook on the side, you might set up a booth for a palm, crystal ball, tarot or Moroccan coffee-cup reader.

The theme "1001 nights" denotes mystery, seduction and drama. It's as evocative and sultry as any veiled beauty. Silks and turbans, jewels and undulating hips make "midnight at the oasis" part of the theme.

SERVES 4

Menu

APPETIZER

Roasted Mediterranean Kabob of Jumbo Prawn, Sea Scallop and Chorizo with

PICTURED, WHITE CHOCOLATE CHEESECAKE SOUFFLE TARTS WITH BRULEE TOPPING

INGREDIENTS

CITRUS HORSERADISH MARMALADE:

- 1 8-OZ JAR OF ORANGE MARMALADE
- 2 TBSP LIME JUICE
- ZEST FROM 2 LIMES
- 3 TBSP HORSERADISH

HONEY MARINADE:

- 1 CUP SIMPLE SYRUP (1 CUP WATER AND 1 CUP SUGAR COMBINED AND STIRRED OVER HEAT UNTIL IT COATS A SPOON)
- 1 CUP HONEY
- 2 SHALLOTS, CHOPPED
- JUICE FROM 3 LEMONS
- 2 TSP NUTMEG

KABOBS:

- 8 6-INCH BAMBOO SKEWERS
- 8 JUMBO SHRIMP, PEELED AND DEVEINED
- 8 LARGE SEA SCALLOPS, MUSCLE REMOVED
- 8 DRIED APRICOTS
- 2 LBS CHORIZO SAUSAGE, CUT IN 1 1/2-INCH DISCS
- SALT AND FRESHLY GROUND BLACK PEPPER
- CITRUS HORSERADISH MARMALADE

PREPARATION

Citrus Horseradish Marmalade:

1) Combine all ingredients and refrigerate for at least 3 hours.

Honey Marinade:

1) Combine the simple syrup and honey in a mixing bowl. Add the shallots, lemon juice and nutmeg.

Kabob:

1) Marinate the shrimp and scallops in the honey marinade for 2 hours.

2) On each skewer put 1 shrimp, scallop, apricot and chorizo disc.

3) Brush lightly with extra marinade and grill over medium flame for 5 minutes on each side. Salt and pepper to taste.

4) Serve with citrus horseradish marmalade.

Saffron-Scented Couscous with Confetti Vegetable Flecks

- 1 PACKAGE DRY COUSCOUS
- 4 TSP SAFFRON
- 1 MEDIUM ZUCCHINI
- 1 MEDIUM YELLOW SQUASH
- 1 LARGE RED PEPPER
- SALT AND FRESHLY GROUND BLACK PEPPER

1) Follow directions on couscous package, adding the saffron to the water.

2) Cut zucchini and summer squash in half. Cut each half in half again, yielding 4 long quarters. Remove the seed portion of the center of the vegetable, discard. Delicately slice each piece on the bias and then slice along the skin side 4 more times yielding a total of 16 thin slices. Dice each slice.

3) Cut red pepper in half, removing seeds.

4) Add diced vegetables to couscous and fluff with a fork to combine. Season with salt and pepper to taste.

Cocktail

Casablanca Oasis

1 oz Stoli Oranj
2 oz Captain Morgan's Rum
1 oz Amaretto
Splash lemon juice
Splash fresh lime juice
Splash bitters

Combine ingredients, shake with ice and strain into a champagne glass. Top with champagne. Garnish with an orange wedge or a lemon twist.

Music

•

The Best Arabian Album in theWorld Ever
EMI International

•

Arabia Remixed
EMI International

•

Arabic Groove
Putumayo

•

Bhangra Beat
Naxos World

•

The Rough Guide to Bhangra
World Music Network

•

Monsoon Wedding (soundtrack)
Milan Records

•

Bollywood Flashback
Bally Sagoo/Columbia/U.K.

•

Anoushka
Anoushka Shankar/Angel Classics

•

Ray of Light
Madonna/Warner Brothers

•

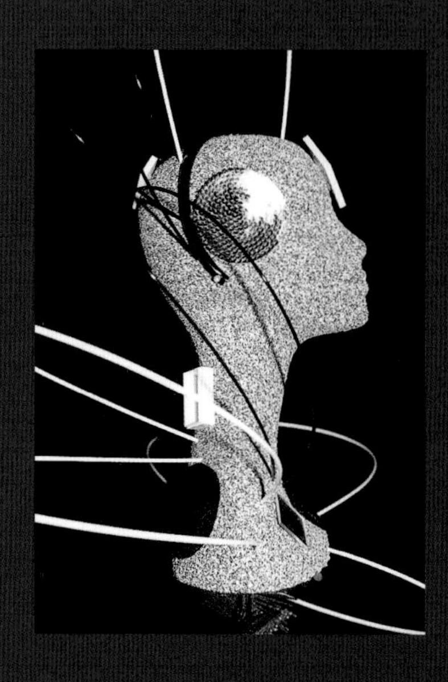

Diner de Têtes

In France, the traditional masquerade party called a "diner de têtes" focuses on everything from the neck up. I remember hearing about a famous Parisian party full of architects and designers who came dressed—heads only—as their favorite buildings or pieces of furniture. In the case of the party thrown here, which we threw for New York's Joseph Papp Public Theater, the focus was not architecture but the theater. Against the backdrop of dark walls and simple, all-black costumes, the highly embellished and richly imagined faces at this party looked wonderful. Think of it, in fact, as a contemporary masquerade—in which grand Venetian-style masks are replaced by, well, absolutely anything you can think of. Here that included silvery green swamp-thing regalia on Pia Getty, a hundred-year-old Medusa crown that came from the costume trunk of Fernanda Niven's grandmother and, for my friend Jeff Klein, a wig full of hideous pink curlers!

10

Dress

The party is different from most in this book because the theme is explicitly non-specific—no one was asked to come as a pirate, for example. It's worth mentioning that non-specificity is both a blessing and a curse. When things are less clear, people have less guidance and are more likely to drop the ball where costumes are concerned. But anything goes, and that's a plus: Guests can pull something together at home—a wig or a silly hat or, in Lulu de Kwiatkowski's case, one tanned cheek painted with leaves.

Invitations

Black provides the base for the dress and décor, and it should do the same for the invitation. Look for very strong contrasts: I recommend intense, nearly fluorescent ink colors such as fuchsia, violet and electric blue and green. To enhance the imagery, focus again on the head: hats, masks, makeup, mirrors, feathers, crowns and headdresses. On a simple black card with bright pink text, include those symbols as decorations to help inspire your guests. Alternately, cut your cards into the shape of hats, or attach a colorful stray feather. I love the idea of an invitation built out of an accordion of different heads, each one black with different headgear.

For a more elaborate invitation—and a more macabre one—send each guest a Styrofoam dummy head (they're very inexpensive), and throw one decorative device in each black cardboard box: paints, glitter, hairpieces, or adhesive crystals or a little mask that your guests can actually wear if they wish. In any case, make sure your guests know to focus on their heads only. Offer them the dress code in a whimsical little poem. My favorite is: "Wear black, just black, all down your back, except for face and hair. Strange hats are fine and masks—divine! Invite your friends to stare."

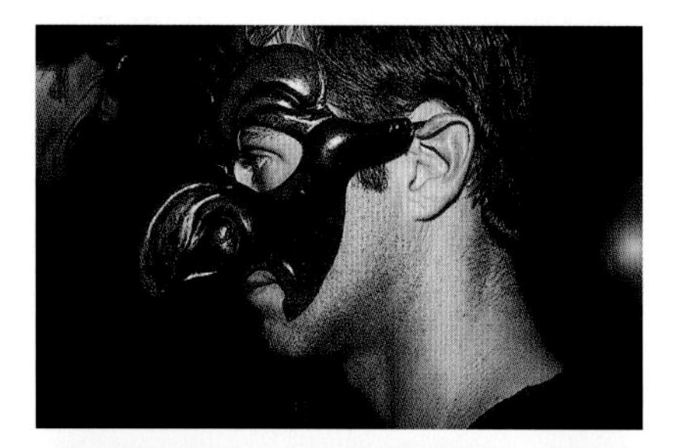

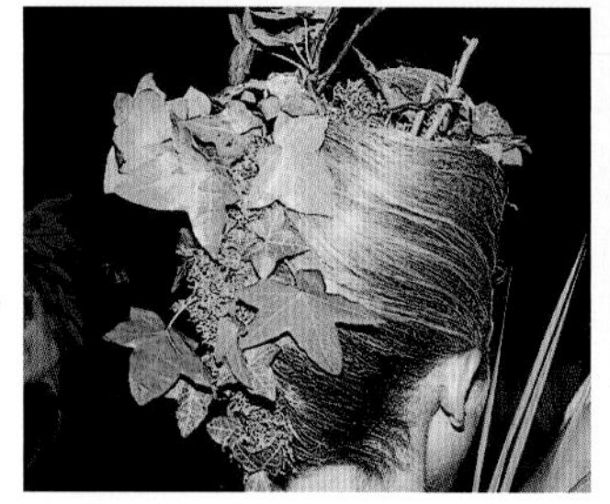

Venue

This theme works well at home for a big party of 40 or more. Have a buffet dinner, confining your decorating to the buffet table since the primary décor of this theme is the guests themselves. A sparsely decorated restaurant, preferably with black walls, is also a good setting for this theme; just make sure that the waiters wear only black. A raw space also works well here: Keep it dim, and use spotlighting to showcase your tables' wacky centerpieces.

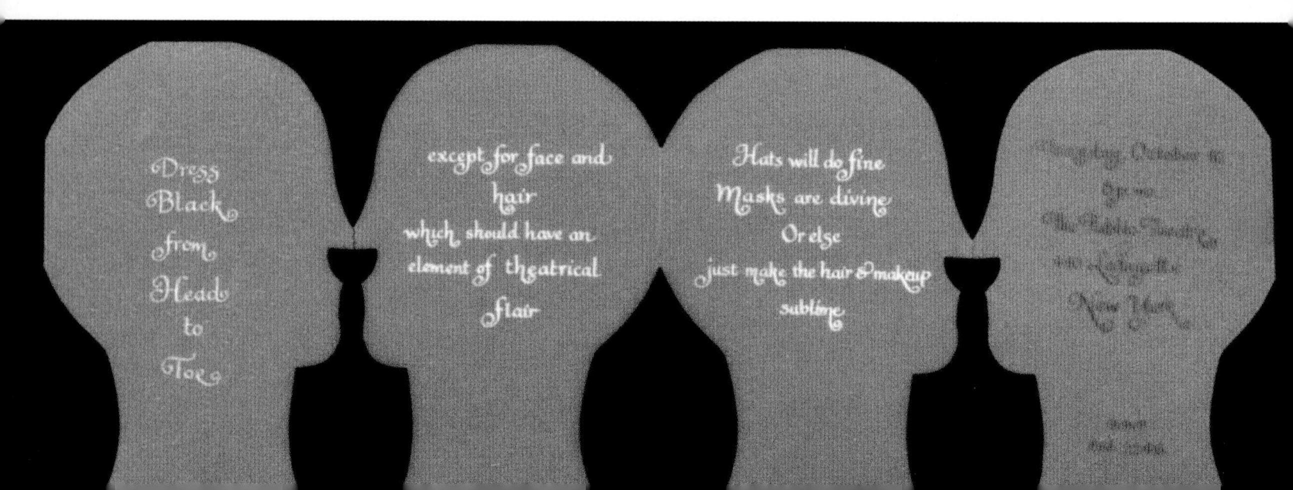

Décor

Keep it simple, focusing on the centerpieces of your spare, black-clothed tables. We used decorated Styrofoam heads, but plaster busts with masks, or sculptures made out of mirrors or illuminated plexiglass, are other good ideas. For the Public Theatre gala shown here—a dinner for two hundred, followed by dancing—we laid the tables with black star-studded tablecloths (a good pun for all the actors in the room). You could use any inexpensive black lamé fabric, however. Bill Tansey, our florist and designer for the event, bought the Styrofoam heads at a mannequin shop and stuck them with ostrich plumes, fluorescent rubber tubes, miniature mirrors and Mylar. He mounted them on pedestals to create absurdist sculptures for the center of each table. We used frosted platters and topped them with black diamond-shaped plates and black napkins. For the place cards, we wrote guests' names in lipstick on small rectangular mirrors.

Entertainment

There's no strict rule for the entertainment here, but I recommend hiring a makeup artist or two to add to the fun—and to help dress up any guests who arrived in a less than inspired costume. This party might also benefit from a caricaturist, someone who will spoof the already overblown faces of your guests. I found one on a walk through Central Park. Karaoke is a terrific idea here too—especially to the classics of musicals. Everyone knows the words to *Guys and Dolls* or *Oklahoma!* and to have the chance to sing these songs is a delight.

No one turned to stone looking at this Medusa in feathers, but Pig-face might need both drinks to make amends for that mug. Putting one's best face forward (one's best mask forward, really) gives this party its theatrical flair.

SERVES 4

Menu

APPETIZER

Goat Cheese Bundles
and
Spring Salad
with Yellow Lentil
Vinaigrette

INGREDIENTS

GOAT CHEESE BUNDLES:
- 2 MEDIUM-SIZED ZUCCHINI
- 1/2 CUP OLIVE OIL
- 1/4 CUP BALSAMIC VINEGAR
- SALT AND FRESHLY GROUND BLACK PEPPER
- 1 LOG MONTRACHET CHEVRE CHEESE

YELLOW LENTIL VINAIGRETTE
- 1 BAG YELLOW LENTILS
- 5 TBSP RED WINE VINEGAR
- 5 TBSP STRONG DIJON MUSTARD
- 1 SHALLOT, CHOPPED
- 1/3 CUP VIRGIN OLIVE OIL
- SALT AND FRESHLY GROUND BLACK PEPPER

SALAD:
- 2 HEADS BUTTER LETTUCE
- 4 ENDIVE
- 3 BUNCH ARUGULA
- 1 PT SUNFLOWER SPROUTS

PREPARATION

Goat Cheese Bundles:
1) Slice zucchini lengthwise about 1/3-inch thick, creating 8 long strips. Toss with olive oil and vinegar, lightly dust with salt and pepper.
2) Grill strips of zucchini for 3 minutes on each side. Cool.
3) Cut the goat cheese into 8 medallions of equal size.
4) Gently wrap zucchini strips around the goat cheese. Refrigerate for 2 hours.

Yellow Lentil Vinaigrette:
1) Prepare lentils, following directions on package. Set aside 1/8 cup cooked lentils.
2) In a bowl, whisk vinegar and Dijon mustard, add chopped shallot. Slowly drizzle in olive oil while whisking. Add salt and pepper to taste.
3) Add to cooked lentils and let sit for 1 hour.

Salad:
1) Wash all lettuces, dry and toss in bowl.
2) Add vinaigrette to desired coating, toss and arrange in a tangle on plate. Garnish with reserved yellow lentils and sunflower sprouts and serve with the goat cheese bundles.

Cocktail

Brazilian Casting Couch

2 oz light rum
Splash fresh lemon juice
Dash sugar
Freshly muddled mint

Combine ingredients, shake with ice, pour into a champagne glass and top with champagne. Garnish with a sprig of fresh mint.

Music

•

Best of Broadway
Rhino
•
Ultimate Broadway
Arista
•
Beautiful Girls
RCA
•
There's No Business Like Show Business
Casablanca
•
Cabaret
Liza Minnelli/MCA
•
Girl Crazy
George & Ira Gershwin
Elektra/Nonesuch
•

Southampton Luau

If there's one American theme party that simply doesn't get enough play, it's the luau. The word evokes the kind of serene, jingly hedonism—decadent but utterly casual—that American city-dwellers so rarely manage to capture at their parties (even their beach parties). The luau invites a multiplicity of variations, and you can aim for the atmosphere and food of a Jamaican, Haitian or Balinese party instead, but the important common requirement is that your party be totally tropical, from soup to macadamia nuts. A real luau, of course, revolves around the roasting and eating of a giant pig. Now, Marjorie Gubelmann, who hosted the party shown here, is an American girl through and through and she wasn't sure that a big porker twirling on a stick would work for her crowd. And, as anyone who's been to a Hamptons dinner party knows, the presence of a little grass or sand isn't always enough to loosen the ties of folks just in from the city.

But Marjorie knows how to have fun: She absolutely insisted on florid, tropical dress (and has the kind of friends who are all too happy to comply), and she filled her chosen restaurant with those tiki torches that make everyone feel sexy and want to behave just a little bit badly! In the end, Marjorie managed to throw a luau that was just exotic enough to transport her flower-decked guests, and at the same time was perfectly matched to their Lily Pulitzer pants and to the genteel character of Southampton, Long Island.

Dress

Island chic, of course—which means head-to-toe hula costume or simply floral prints, sarongs, one-shoulder dresses and flowers in the hair for women, and Hawaiian shirts, white trousers or Bermuda shorts for the men. At Marjorie's party, Lily Pulitzer, the queen of seventies Palm Beach style, was especially popular, as were the glamorous summer dresses of Emilio Pucci and Emanuel Ungaro.

Invitation

The luau immediately brings to mind grass skirts and hula dancers, palm trees and coconuts, orchids and pineapples. Chromatically, I like to combine bright greens, oranges and pinks (the colors of Hawaiian hibiscus bushes) on this invitation. But it's very easy to do more than just the standard card here: I suggest sending each person a pineapple or a mini-palm with a card attached, or just a simple silk lei from the party store. If you're having your invitations hand-delivered, you might also buy some giant leaves from your florist and inscribe them with party details using a gold pen. Marjorie had an even better idea: She found electronic, grass-skirted Barbie-size dolls that dance the hula at the press of a button. Every guest got one with the invitation attached.

Venue

The beach, of course, is the ideal location for this party. But a flower-strewn lawn will work fine, or a pool turned into an island oasis. Marjorie threw her luau at Southampton's Club Colette, whose umbrella-lined porch became a Hawaiian beach hut with the help of a few palm fronds and paper lanterns.

Décor

Whether you're throwing the party at the beach or elsewhere, mix torchlight with candlelight (for the drama of the former and the soft intimacy of the latter). And if you need to, bring the beach inside: Strew your tent with sand, fill it with orchids, palms and baskets of tropical fruit, and put a table's worth of leis by the entrance—Marjorie's were made of fresh orchids, FedExed from Hawaii to arrive that day. For escort cards, I like to split coconuts, fill them with a mai tai cocktail and install little straws with flags attached that bear the name and table of each guest.

Name each table after a tropical locale: Tahiti, St. Croix, Kawai, Seychelles, Trinidad. Tablecloths made of raffia or other grass-skirting material provide a touch of humor—not to mention some textural interest—but white cloths always look wonderful against the tropical flora. Replicating the lushness of the tropics as best you can is the key here. Bamboo candlesticks, which can be purchased inexpensively at Pier I Imports, keep the table light soft. Scatter each place with sand and small shells (which, by the way, look wonderful spray-painted pink, green or gold), and be sure to put one giant, lush orchid in a pool of water beside every woman's place so she can wear it in her hair after dinner.

Entertainment

Hula dancers, in grass skirts and coconut bras, are the perfect entertainers here. But reggae and steel bands work well too—remember that the sound of the marimba is a powerful auditory cue—and so do those languid, loungy Hawaiian-music records from the sixties that you can buy at flea markets. And on the dance floor: limbo (for which you should have a prize planned for the Queen of the Luau—maybe one of those Swarovski crystal pineapples?).

Dark jackets... and grass skirts! Even your most uptight friends can don leis and let their hair down for this tropical paradise party. Whether the shore is 100 miles away or in your backyard, this "leid"-back atmosphere of a beach at dusk will transform your guests: If only for a night!

SERVES 5

Menu

APPETIZER

INGREDIENTS

PREPARATION

Saki Shrimp

- 1 POUND ATLANTIC JUMBO SHRIMP IN THE SHELL
- 2 CUPS SAKI
- 2 TBSP OLD BAY SEASONING

1) Shell and devein shrimp.
2) In a bowl, combine saki and seasoning.
3) Place shrimp in a shallow saucepan and pour seasoning mixture over it.
4) Cover saucepan and cook over medium heat. When the water comes to a boil, turn heat down to low and simmer until shrimp is done, about 4 minutes, or until firm and just cooked through.
5) Remove from liquid and cool.

Spring Rolls (makes 10)

- 3 TBSP VEGETABLE OIL
- 1 TBSP MINCED GARLIC
- 1/2 TBSP GRATED GINGER
- 2 CUPS FINELY SHREDDED CHINESE CABBAGE
- 1 CARROT, GRATED
- 1/2 CUP BEAN SPROUTS
- 8 OZ COOKED, SHREDDED PORK
- 1 TBSP LIGHT SOY SAUCE
- 1 TBSP OYSTER SAUCE
- 2 TBSP CHOPPED CILANTRO
- 1 TSP SALT
- 1 PACKAGE SPRING ROLL WRAPPERS

1) Heat vegetable oil in a skillet or a wok over high heat.
2) Add the garlic, ginger, cabbage, carrot and bean sprouts. Cook until the cabbage becomes limp, about 2 minutes.
3) Add pork, raise the heat and stir fry until it changes color.
4) Stir in the soy and oyster sauces, toss to coat thoroughly.
5) Remove from heat and cool. Add chopped cilantro and a pinch of salt.
6) Place a spring roll wrapper on a flat surface, spoon 2 tablespoons of the filling at one end of the wrapper and roll up half way on the diagonal. Fold in the two sides, dampen edges with water and continue rolling to form a tight roll. Press the edges to seal.
7) Heat the remaining tablespoon of oil in a skillet at 350°F. Fry one or two at a time in the hot oil, turning to cook all sides until golden brown, about 2 minutes for each.

Cocktail

Mai Tai

3 oz Bacardi 8
1 oz apricot brandy
1 oz pineapple juice
Splash almond liqueur
Splash fresh lime juice

Combine ingredients, shake and pour over ice into a daiquiri glass. Garnish with fresh fruit. (Umbrella optional.)

Music

•

Greetings from Hawaii
Laserlight
•

Quiet Village, The Enchanted Sea
Martin Denny/Scamp
•

The Exotic Moods of Les Baxter
Les Baxter/Capitol
•

Steel Drum Favorites
Laserlight
•

Ultra Lounge/Tiki Sampler
Capitol
•

Skyscraper Garden Luncheon

Who says you can't have a peaceful garden lunch right in the middle of New York City, even when there's not a patch of green grass in sight? A quiet rooftop terrace, glass-enclosed porch or well-planted terrarium can easily morph into a noon-time oasis—one whose concrete floor won't stain a new pair of heels. This theme works best for a springtime ladies' luncheon, and if you live in the city, as I do, you and your friends will love the playful irony of a roomful of a sherbet-attired women in hats fit for the races, standing atop a 30-story building.

Décor

Sad to say, this theme forces you to confront the worst of all possible lighting—daylight! If it's very warm, just be sure there's enough shade to keep the sun in check; no one wants to sweat through lunch, except, perhaps, on the beach. I like to keep the palette of this party as froufrou as possible just for the fun of it: pastels, citrus fruit and apricots, paper butterflies. For the party featured here, I had the good fortune to have access to Christofle's fabulous tableware, but any elegant white porcelain, preferably rimmed in gold or silver to complement the flowers, will do; pastel-colored plates are too much. For a party of 16, a square table with four people to a side is a better bet than a round or rectangular table. Decorate it with loads of flowers, colorful goblets and sugar-coated almonds in silver bowls.

For some whimsy, I asked each of my guests to send me a photograph of her children in advance. Then I put the pictures in little silver frames and used them as placecards in lieu of the mothers' names. (For a birthday, you might do this with baby pictures of the guests themselves.) It can be a bit of a headache to trim every photo to fit the picture frames—but when you see the smiles they bring to the faces of your guests, you'll know it was worth it.

Dress

Garden party attire, of course—floral or pastel dresses and suits with hats.

Invitations

For a garden luncheon in the city, you should aim for an invitation that plays with the contrasts between city and country. For the party featured here, I commissioned a card whose outside flap was a gray cutout of the Manhattan skyline with an interior floral pattern of baby blues and greens peeking out from underneath. There are other ways to emphasize the dichotomy: Send a small arrangement of flowers in a cubic cement pot cut from a cinderblock, or lay a bouquet of hybrid gray roses inside a pale green box. Alternately, send a miniature paper hat—available at any party store—bearing the invite.

Venue

Consider yourself lucky if you can find a terrace or winter garden with sprawling city views, but keep in mind that any small city garden, in the back of a brownstone or in the courtyard of an apartment building, will adapt nicely to this theme. If none of these is available, do it at home or in a restaurant, as long as you manage to focus attention inward to the flowers, vines and blush hues of the table.

In these informal hectic days when city-dwellers forget there's a color called green, a tranquil afternoon ode to the garden feels just right. Bringing an airy garden party to the urban jungle can be quite a feat, but the flowers, hats and silver go a long way toward restoring one's sense of calm within the urban storm.

Entertainment You may opt for the gentle musings of a pianist (I find strings or a chamber group a bit pretentious for a lunch among friends). But other than light background music, no entertainment is necessary here.

SERVES 4

Menu

MAIN COURSE

Pepper-Crusted Seared Tuna Salad with Asian Vinaigrette

INGREDIENTS

- 1/4 CUP AGED RICE WINE VINEGAR
- 1 TBSP SOY SAUCE
- JUICE OF 1/2 LIME
- 1 TSP GRATED GINGER
- 1/2 CUP CANOLA OIL
- 1 LB TUNA LOIN, CUT INTO 4 STRIPS
- 1 TSP SALT
- 2 TBSP SZECHUAN PEPPER, FRESHLY GROUND
- 1 TBSP EXTRA VIRGIN OLIVE OIL
- 3 CARROTS, GRATED
- 3 CUCUMBERS, SLICED INTO 1/8-INCH WIDE, 2-INCH LONG STRIPS
- 2 SCALLIONS, DICED
- 1 BUNCH RADISH SPROUTS
- 1 BUNCH CILANTRO

PREPARATION

1) In a bowl whisk together the vinegar, soy sauce, lime juice and ginger. Slowly pour in the canola oil while whisking.
2) Season the tuna with salt and Szechuan pepper on all sides.
3) In large skillet heat olive oil over high heat until just smoking. Sear the tuna strips on all sides until cooked rare, about 30 seconds per side. Remove from pan and slice each piece into approx. 4 1/2-inch thick slices.
4) Divide the grated carrots, cucumbers, scallions and radish sprouts between four plates, place 4 slices of tuna on each and drizzle with the vinaigrette. Garnish with a few leaves of cilantro and serve.

Cocktail

Lunch Lemonade

4 oz gin
Sprite and lemon juice (equal parts)
Dash of sugar

Combine ingredients, shake and pour over ice into a highball glass. Garnish with a lemon wheel. (Can be made without gin for a refreshing alternative.)

Music

•

Classical Chillout
Angel
•

Debussy Dreams
EMI Classics
•

Satie Works for Piano
EMI Classics
•

Classical Dreams Music to Inspire
Virgin Classics
•

Written in the Stars
Bill Charlap/Blue Note
•

Up on the Roof
Under the Boardwalk
The Drifters/Collectibles
•

A Day Without Rain
Enya/Warner Brothers
•

Black and White . . . and Diamonds

Of course, Truman Capote set the standard for this theme at his legendary ball in November 1966. Like that famous party, there will be no shades of gray here. It's an easy yet elegant theme, and the more people you invite—Capote had 540—the more brilliant the effect. Inevitably, the theme summons to mind the monochromatic thirties Hollywood glamour of MGM movies like *Grand Hotel*, the high-deco magic of the Chrysler building, the zebra banquettes of El Morocco and the Cubist paintings of Juan Gris. Yet black and white always feels wonderfully modern, if occasionally a bit cold. That's why I like to warm up the theme with a little...ice! Invite your guests to lay on their diamonds (women always want an excuse to wear them), and you'll see what a gaudy, glittery difference it makes.

My friends Kalliope Karella and Anne McNally and I threw the dinner featured here for Chanel, the holy French fashion house. It was the perfect theme for a company that built its reputation on the little black dress. We took over their New York headquarters on 57th Street, serving cocktails in the boutique and dinner in a banquet room high above.

Dress

This theme begs for formal attire: Black-tie or a playful variation thereof for the men, and for women, white stoles, hair up, glamour to the nines! But there's no reason not to have other kinds of fun with this theme. Encourage your guests to spray their hair black and white in the spirit of Deeda Blair. I like the idea of Playboy bunnies—some in black, some in white—as bartenders or wait staff. Keep in mind, too, that with some fake cobwebs and rubber spiders, this theme would work beautifully for an opulent Halloween dinner.

Invitations

As long as you stick to its basic principle, this theme allows for infinite variation. Use black-and-white patterned paper, write on the back of some vintage photographs from the flea market, glue white feathers to a black card, send out two roses (one black, one white) or even deliver those black-and-white half-moon cookies with a card attached. We sent out simple black sparkly cards printed with black ink, but you might also use acetate sheets, which you can trim into the shape of a king-cut diamond if you wish. If you're adding diamonds to your theme, attach some tiny crystals to your card, or, better still, send each couple or female guest a crystal tiara or necklace bearing the party notice.

Venue

The key to this theme is simplicity: You want a spare, monochromatic space—black or white—against which your guests' glamorous dresses will pop out. Keep it slick and sleek, but don't rule out a checkerboard marble hall, or even a skating rink! Just imagine your friends trading their heels for blades, and the spectacle of black and white fur coats floating over the ice.

Décor

As with the theme, the only rule here is contrast. I recommend a dinner party with two tables—one black, one white. You'll see here that the Chanel dinner tables were set in opposites: Event Quest set black plates and white napkins tied with black feathers on one, white plates and black napkins tied with white gardenias on the other. If you like, play with the theme's connotations of good and evil in the centerpieces: Guests will enjoy the angel in the middle of their table and the devil in the middle of the neighbors'. To reinforce the glittering effect of diamonds, use cut-crystal glassware and scatter the tables with tiny crystals or white glitter. Think about keeping everything geometric: Square chargers and dishes, rectilinear flower arrangements, flickering cubic votives everywhere.

Entertainment

The old-fashioned glitz of this theme calls for jazz above all, but a fifties cover band would also work during the cocktail hour. For dinner and dancing, ask your favorite deejay to dress all in white and mix his set with a few jazz-age chestnuts. During dinner, consider asking a magician to wander between tables performing simple tricks.

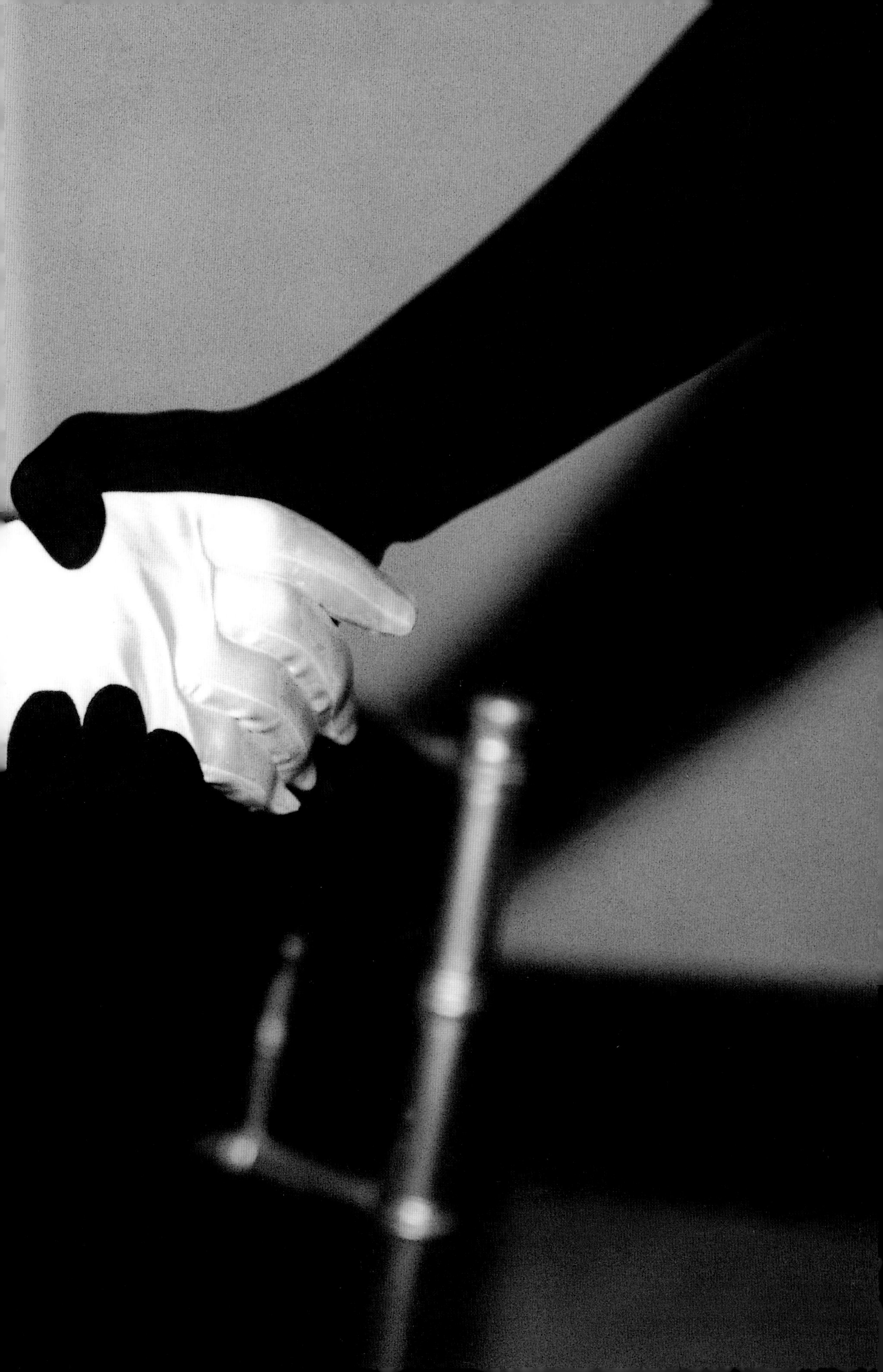

These beautiful creatures dripping with diamonds could just as easily have walked out of a Cole Porter tune as out of that pinnacle of sophistication, Chanel in New York City. But elegant black and white can work anywhere—even if Tiffany isn't on your block.

SERVES 4

Menu

APPETIZER

Sevruga Caviar on Potato Crisps with Crème Fraîche

INGREDIENTS

- 1 NEW POTATO
- 1 TBSP BLENDED OIL
- SALT AND FRESHLY GROUND BLACK PEPPER
- 1 OZ SEVRUGA CAVIAR
- 1 OZ CRÈME FRAÎCHE OR SOUR CREAM
- 3 CHIVES (OPTIONAL)
- 1 SPRIG DILL (OPTIONAL)

PREPARATION

1) Scrub potato well and slice very thinly on a mandoline into 10 to 15 thin slices.
2) Toss slices with the oil, salt and pepper.
3) Place potato slices on a metal baking sheet, brush with butter, and place another baking sheet on top to keep potatoes very flat.
4) Roast in a 350°F oven for approximately 10 minutes, until golden brown and crispy.
5) Top potato crisps with a dab of crème fraîche (or sour cream) and a dollop of caviar.
6) Garnish with chive tip or dill sprig, if desired.

Cocktail

Dark and White Chocolate Martinis

2 oz Kremylovskaya chocolate vodka
2 oz Godiva dark or white chocolate liqueur

Combine ingredients, shake with ice and strain into a chilled martini glass. (Glass rim can be lined with sugar or cocoa.)

Music

•

Night and Day
The Cole Porter/Songbook/Polygram
•

Ballads
Cannonball Adderley/Blue Note
•

Something Cool
June Christy /Blue Note
•

The Romantic Moods of Jackie Gleason
Capitol
•

Lush Life
Nat King Cole/Blue Note
•

The Best of the Songbooks The Ballads
Ella Fitzgerald/Polygram
•

After Hours
Sarah Vaughan/Blue Note
•

Pretty in Pink

The party pictured here is a baby shower—a baby shower for me, in fact, which took place shortly before the birth of my second daughter, Talia. The typical baby shower is a luncheon or a tea, but in my mind that's just the sort of sleepy convention that would make a "dinner-in-pink" both surprising and fun.

Of course, you can adapt this concept to blue for a boy, or pink and blue for a child of unknown gender. And why not flout tradition even more? A perfectly viable, if not exactly classical, way to inject some novelty into a party that so often verges on the overly precious is to bring the men in. I've had great fun at mixed showers where women come all in pink and men come all in blue.

Invitations

My friends Cristina Tabet and Serena Boardman threw this party for me, and Cristina made the invitations on her home computer using pale pink cards printed with a stork she found on a disk of clip art. She asked people to dress "pretty in pink"—a notion that tends to provoke either delight, nausea, or a combination of both. Fortunately, my friends got into the spirit (thank goodness for Tory Burch, who has an incredible collection of vintage pink dresses!). For a boy's shower, invite your friends to dress as "blue belles." You can also use lilac as the theme's dominant color—it's a little different and works for baby girls and boys.

An adorable alternative to a simple card is to order T-shirts printed with the party details, rolled and stuffed into individual baby bottles and sent by mail. (You can also print the front with the name of the honoree and ask your friends to wear them to the event—then you've got an adorable photo-op.) A printed bib or a little stuffed stork, whose pouch contains the invitation, are other cute options here. If you have a messenger service at your disposal, consider sending individual pink cupcakes with the invitations written in icing; in New York, we've got an embarrassment of fantastic little cupcake shops to choose from.

Décor

Though most people throw showers at home, any restaurant or raw space can be transformed for the event with balloons, pink or blue, covering the ceiling, with long colorful ribbons attached. The only rule here is to stick to the color. Pink balloons actually filter and reflect light beautifully, so you'll be surprised at how rosy things look by simply flooding a room with them. Tie babies' bibs to your champagne bottles; put pink flowers everywhere (no pink roses, please, they're unquestionably the Pepto-Bismol of the flower kingdom!). Teddy bears are always sweet, and Cristina stacked white plates with lattices through which she wove pink ribbons. If you're throwing a buffet at home, a fabulous, rigorously in-theme buffet table is all you need. For a seated lunch, though, consider using inscribed bibs, pacifiers or toy carriages as place cards, and substitute vases full of pink candy for flowers here and there.

Entertainment

At a baby shower, entertainment usually comes in the form of a gift-opening ceremony. I happen to think that opening gifts kills a party; it can get awfully boring for your guests to feel they have to ooh and aah over an interminable run of baby toys and mini-pinafores. For people who don't have children or don't go weak for babies, it can be torture. Not to mention the pressure on the host and the honoree to respond with equal enthusiasm to the most beautiful and the most hideous of gifts—or to handle gracefully receiving two of the same thing! I suggest saving the gift opening for later. Instead, use the party to catch up with friends and have fun: For that purpose, light background music is all you need.

Who says pink has to be prissy? Pink champagne (yes, in baby bottles) sets the tone for a festive shower that is as sophisticated and relaxed as it is sweet (lots of pink cakes, candies and fruit) and charming.

Tartine

Music

•

For Our Children
Rhino
•
For Our Children Too
Rhino Records
•
Small Fry
Capitol Sings Kids' Songs for Grownups
Capitol
•
Free To Be You And Me
Marlo Thomas/Arista
•
Parents' Lullaby Album
Angel
•
Classical Dreams
Virgin classics
•

Menu

Unless you find the fifties the most terrifying decade imaginable, you'll want lots of pink food here. There's nothing quite as decadent (and yes, as weird) as a monochromatic buffet spread—but, believe me, a pink-food-only table looks terrific. Cristina served pink champagne in baby bottles instead of flutes, with pink straws to sip through. If you want more of a bang from your bottle, however, try serving watermelon martinis! There were pink frosted cakes and cupcakes, a giant bowl of strawberries, raspberry mousse, pink jellybeans, pink lemonade and pink lollypops. Adults love kiddie food, so for a shower I like to stick to a seven-year-old's menu and not get overly sophisticated. If you wish, you can always serve poached salmon and a beet-radicchio salad. Just keep in mind that women tend to eat very little around tea time, so light, decorative foods (cookies and candies) fit the bill.

Cocktail

Watermelon Martini

3 oz vodka
Fresh muddled watermelon
Dash of sugar

Combine ingredients, shake over ice and serve up in a chilled martini glass (or bottle!). Garnish with a slice of fresh watermelon.

Signature Styles

This theme plays on the word "signature," inviting guests to celebrate all that is signature about themselves—their handwriting, their personality, and above all, their style. I threw the party pictured here at Daniel, the heavenly French restaurant on East 65th Street in New York, along with *Food & Wine* magazine. The idea was to invite New Yorkers with strong and distinct styles to come very much as themselves (as the epitome of themselves, in fact) and to sit down to a dinner of signature dishes of four world-class chefs. What's unique about this party is that it asks the guests not to become someone else, as on most themed occasions, but simply to come as they really, truly are: There's only one Nan Kempner, for example, so leave it to Nan to arrive wearing Yves Saint Laurent couture, the stuff she's worn on big nights since the seventies! Of course, signature doesn't have to be quite so over-the-top; my friend Serena Boardman invariably wears a sleeveless A-line shift dress. Serena has this dress in every color and every fabric, and wears one regardless of the weather or the look of the moment. It was a pleasure to see her walk in looking so much herself!

Visually, this party was a play on words: We used the rather library-like private room at the restaurant, and filled it with all the rich symbols of the writing life—plumes and quills, ink wells, parchment, leather and suede and the earthy tones of the study in which John Hancock might have signed his own John Hancock.

Décor

To enhance the sense of scholarly coziness, we decorated with globes in addition to flowers, brass-rimmed magnifying glasses on the place settings and blotters in lieu of place mats. This party offers an opportunity to work out a very masculine scheme: suede tablecloths (ultrasuede, in our case), wooden candlesticks, bowls of nuts.

At a Philadelphia souvenir shop, Dana Cowin, the editor in chief of *Food & Wine*, found parchment printed with the Declaration of Independence. We wrapped it around our votives so the old cursive would glow from within.

We also found wrapping paper printed with famous signatures, which we laid across a table by the door where we'd propped a guest book along with a pen and ink. (If any party warrants a guest book, it's this one!)

Dress

This party is meant to be a celebration of everything that's distinctive about your guests. My old friend Tiffany Dubin, who always looks like she just stepped out of the most perfectly preserved time capsule, wore a Courrèges dress from the sixties. Jonathan Adler, the New York home designer, wore Lacoste—as always. Amy Fine Collins, the fashion writer for *Vanity Fair*, wore Geoffrey Beene (she's his muse, after all), and Nina Griscom, the food writer, wore Bill Blass just as she has for the past two decades. Then there was Nan: "This is from Yves's last collection," she said of her black tuxedo. "It's so Yves, it's me. And it's so me, it's Yves."

Venue

This party, as I've imagined it, calls for a cozy library—but "signature" is a fertile word, and there are countless other possibilities. Create a signature room of your own: for example, if you love fur, do a furry room, if you love Tiffany lamps, do a Tiffany lamp room—whatever describes you. Or, if you're a fashion and decorating maven, hang or place signature clothing and objects throughout the party space. I personally like neutral ground because it doesn't privilege any one of the night's signatures over another. Food was very much the focus of the party shown here, so we made the table the focal point of the evening. Because it's a theme that really only works for people with very strong personal styles, you're probably going to want to keep this party rather small; a dinner at home or in an intimate room at a restaurant makes the most sense.

Invitations

Take advantage of the literary symbolism invoked by the library décor. Write the invitations in the rich, irregular arabesques of a fountain pen, allowing for picturesque drops and blurs. Seal the envelope with wax.

For our signature party, we created an invitation box filled with signature-related items: a maroon quill pen, a note card decorated with shorthand writing and a return envelope with an Arabic calligraphy stamp. In the box, the invitation came with a somewhat intensive set of instructions: First, guests were asked to write their signatures on a card and mail them back; next, guests were asked to write out the following sentence on a blank card and return it in the accompanying envelope: "Now is the time for all great men to come to the aid of their country."

After collecting the invitees' signatures, we sent them to Karen Charatan, a lettering artist, who applied each guest's signature to a napkin. The process isn't so difficult: Karen placed a cotton-blend napkin on a light box (only cotton-blend napkins will do as they prevent the ink from bleeding), then she traced each signature with a fabric marker.

Meanwhile, we forwarded the writing samples to a handwriting analyst, and printed each analysis (lighthearted, mind you) along with the menus that stood at each guest's place.

I

What could be more fun than going to a party as your favorite person—yourself! The more of you, the better. Guests here had no harder task than to wow the crowd with the gifts that flow naturally.

MAKES 3-DOZEN HORS D'ŒUVRES

Menu

If you're doing a dinner at home, then it almost goes without saying that you should whip up your own signature dishes. This is one theme for which a potluck makes a lot of sense, too—not to mention being surprising and fun. Ask each of your guests to bring their own signature dish (but be sure to coordinate to ensure a balanced dinner) The menu here comes from four of New York's most celebrated chefs: Nobu Matsuhisa of Nobu, Daniel Boulud of Daniel, Terrence Brennan of Picholine and Artisanal, and Claudia Fleming of Gramercy Tavern.

APPETIZER

Mushroom Pomponnettes (see bottom photo) Adapted by Food & Wine magazine, from Daniel Boulud

INGREDIENTS

PASTRY:

- 1 CUP ALL-PURPOSE FLOUR
- 6 TBSP UNSALTED BUTTER, CUT INTO PIECES AND CHILLED
- 1/8 TSP SALT
- 1 LARGE EGG, LIGHTLY BEATEN

FILLING:

- 1 CUP DRIED PORCINI MUSHROOMS
- 2 CUPS BOILING WATER
- 1 TBSP UNSALTED BUTTER
- 1 TBSP EXTRA-VIRGIN OLIVE OIL
- 1 GARLIC CLOVE, MINCED
- 1 TBSP FLAT-LEAF PARSLEY, FINELY CHOPPED
- 1/2 CUP HEAVY CREAM
- 1 LARGE EGG
- 1 LARGE EGG YOLK
- 1/2 CUP SHREDDED FONTINA CHEESE
- 1 TBSP SNIPPED CHIVES
- SALT AND PEPPER

PREPARATION

Pastry:

1) In a food processor, mix flour, butter and salt. Pour beaten egg evenly over mixture and stir several times. Flatten pastry into a disc, wrap and refrigerate at least 30 minutes.
2) Preheat oven to 350°F. On a lightly floured surface, roll pastry into a 14-inch round circle 1/4-inch thick. Using a 2-inch round cookie cutter, stamp out as many rounds as possible.
3) Line cups of three 12-cup mini-muffin pans with pastry rounds, pressing pastry into molds. Refrigerate until firm.
4) Cut out 36 2-inch squares of foil and line pastry with them. Bake for 15 minutes or until shells are dry. Remove foil and let cool.

Filling:

1) In a heatproof medium bowl, soak porcini in boiling water until softened, about 20 minutes. Lift out of water and pat dry. Then chop the porcini finely.
2) In a medium skillet, melt butter in the olive oil. When foam subsides, add porcini and cook over medium-high heat, stirring until golden, about 3 minutes. Add garlic and cook until fragrant, about 1 minute. Season with salt and pepper to taste and stir in parsley.
3) Transfer mixture to a bowl and let cool, then whisk in the cream, whole egg, egg yolk and Fontina.

1) Spoon mushroom custard into pastry shells and sprinkle with chives.
2) Bake at 350°F for about 15 minutes, or until set. Let pomponnettes cool slightly before serving.

Baked pomponnettes can be refrigerated overnight and rewarmed in a 325°F oven.

Cocktail

Signature Valentino

2 oz Stoli Strasberi
Splash passion fruit puree
Splash grenadine
Splash sugar

Combine ingredients, shake with ice and pour into a champagne glass. Top with champagne and garnish with a halved strawberry.

Music

•

Velvet Underground & Nico
The Velvet Underground
Polygram

•

La vie en rose
Edith Piaf/Asv living Era

•

Flirting with Twilight
Kurt Elling/Blue note

•

The Very Best of Marvin Gaye
Universal

•

Sinatra Reprise
The Very Good Years
Warner Brothers

•

Bobby Darin
The Hit Singles Collection
Rhino

•

Walking on Thin Ice
Yoko Ono/Rykodisc

•

Scent of a Woman

When Saks Fifth Avenue asked me to organize a theme party around the launch of Oscar de la Renta's new perfume (provocatively named *Intrusion*), I looked for a subject that would celebrate the particular and highly elegant mystique of Oscar himself—while promising a great deal of fun for his guests. I began to think about *Scent of a Woman*, the 1992 remake of the 1974 Italian film of the same name. In the newer version, Al Pacino plays a war hero whose blindness impels him to use his sense of smell when hunting for love. It's a darkly romantic story, and one that exalts womanliness in much the same way that Oscar—the designer who knows better than any other how a woman wants to feel when she puts a dress on—has done over his 35-year career.

The film is also laced with the languorous strains of the tango (in its most famous scene, Pacino teaches a very young Chris O'Donnell how to dance one), and of course Oscar has often conjured the dance in his ruffled skirts and peasant tops. In the end, we threw a party that brought the shadowy drama of an Argentine tango bar into harmony with a celebration of summer.

Dress

The simple dress code—ruffles and florals—set the tone here: Most women already have a dress in their closet, worn not often enough, that makes them feel especially feminine (and maybe just a little naughty, too). Faced with a sea of naked shoulders and skirts that open like umbrellas when they spin, the men in the crowd all begin to share in the spirit of Pacino's hungry hunter.

Invitations

We wanted to make an immediate appeal to my guests' sense of smell, which is why we sent each of them a single fragrant gardenia in a small pot. Inspired by a particular dress from one of Oscar's collections, we chose lime green as the thematic color of the party; accordingly, we tied a card to each flowerpot on which the party details were written in lime-green ink. Fresh flowers aren't very easy to manage (you might do a boxed paper flower instead—and write the invitation out on the unfurled petals), but another way to capitalize on the allure of a particular scent is to send each guest a small potpourri sachet—based upon the color or flower around which you'll plan your décor.

Lavender is a wonderful tone and a wonderful scent for this party; consider sending a purple pouchful tied to a card, or simply slip a sprig into each envelope along with the invitation. Any fresh, summery colors will work well with this theme—and a good way to encourage your guests to wear their most tango-worthy dresses is to buy a sheet of fabric in your chosen color and glue three rectangular pieces, overlapping slightly, on the back of each invitation card to create a billowing, ruffled little teaser.

Venue

This theme works perfectly as a garden party, or in a conservatory, greenhouse or sunroom filled with fragrant flowers. we looked for a room that would befit the glamour of Oscar de la Renta, with high ceilings, swirling moldings and crystal chandeliers—and we found it at the Americas Society, a New York foundation that supports cultural exchange among North, Central and South America.

The cocktail hour took place in a wood-paneled library, after which guests floated into the beautiful dining room whose lime-colored walls gleamed like cake frosting.

A celebration of all that is feminine and lovely, fragrant and alluring. Opulent flowers and their heady scents fill the air, culminating in the sexiest dance of dances—the tango.

Décor

One of my favorite dresses in Oscar's spring collection was a delicious tango fantasia that united a white eyelet bustier and a lime-green ruffled skirt, its waist cinched with hot-pink satin ribbon. I decided that these elements would make the perfect dinner table, so Oscar adapted the dress into a chartreuse-colored cloth that ruffled down to the floor and overlaid it with white eyelet; hot-pink ribbons to tie the napkins completed the homage. There were seven tables at the party—each intended to give visual, as well as olfactory, expression to one of the seven elements used in Oscar's new fragrance.

The centerpieces, too, were composed around those elements: A dramatic puff of white peonies floated over the middle of one table; graceful lilies danced in the center of another, and decorative glass containers in various sizes filled with perfumed mounds of star anise studded a third. The table called "Amber" (named for the aromatic resin that forms the stone) was adorned with strands of amber beads of different shapes and sizes winding through amber-colored pillar candles. An herb table, meanwhile, was redolent of the herb topiaries and delicate herb clusters that decorated it. On top of the basic color scheme, the seven tables were unified by the use of glittering beige votives covered in skeleton leaves, and white floating candles in delicate celadon glasses.

Regardless of the kind of party you're throwing, tables differentiated by scent—rose, jasmine, tiger lily—can be a wonderful way to celebrate the summer (especially if you have a fragrant garden of your own from which to pluck your flowers). Lay a flower at the place of each of your female guests so she can put it in her hair before rising to dance. Food purists, who believe that no fragrance should overpower the one rising from the dinner plates, may be appalled by all this flower power. But never mind them; in my opinion, a host can do nothing better than stimulate as many of the senses as possible.

Entertainment

Most people love the tango as much as they're terrified by it. So for the party shown here, we hired a pair of tango instructors to weave through the crowd offering an informal lesson in the dance's basic steps. In general, hiring a dance instructor for the afternoon or evening provides wonderfully original entertainment at a party: For a Jazz Age affair, you might hire someone to teach the Charleston, for a Big Band Forties party you could resurrect the Lindy hop, for a Latin party you might have a dancer or two on hand to give a salsa lesson. To get the fun started, be sure to direct your dance instructors to those guests who are most outgoing (this will be easy, as they'll probably be the first to get up to dance anyway). We were lucky enough to have the added flavor of a fabulous tango trio whom Oscar de la Renta had invited up from his hometown of Santo Domingo; and in Oscar, we found we had a surprise guest star who grabbed the microphone after dinner and sang alongside his friends.

Menu

SERVES 4

APPETIZER	INGREDIENTS

PREPARATION

Steamed Asparagus with Lemon Tarragon Dressing

- ZEST FROM 1 LEMON
- 3 TBSP LEMON JUICE
- 1 CLOVE GARLIC, FINELY MINCED
- 1/2 TSP SEA SALT
- 1/2 TSP FRESHLY GROUND BLACK PEPPER
- 1 CUP EXTRA VIRGIN OLIVE OIL
- 10 TARRAGON LEAVES, MINCED
- 24 ASPARGUS, PEELED
- ORANGE RIND FOR GARNISH

1) Mix together first five ingredients.
2) Slowly whisk in the olive oil, then add the tarragon and whisk well. Set aside.
3) Steam asparagus approx. 4 minutes until bright green and tender.
4) Drizzle dressing over asparagus and garnish with orange rind.

This recipe can be made a day ahead and refrigerated. Bring to room temperature. .prior to serving.

Passion Fruit Pavlova

MERINGUE:

- 6 EXTRA LARGE EGGS AT ROOM TEMPERATURE, SEPARATED (YOLKS RESERVED FOR FILLING)
- 3/4 TSP CREAM OF TARTAR
- 1 TSP SALT
- 1 1/2 TSP VANILLA
- 1 1/2 CUPS GRANULATED SUGAR

FILLING:

- 1 PACKET KNOX GELATIN
- 3/4 CUP FROZEN PASSION FRUIT PUREE (DEFROSTED)
- 6 EGG YOLKS (WHISKED)
- 3 TBSP ALL-PURPOSE FLOUR
- 1 1/2 CUPS GRANULATED SUGAR
- 1/4 TSP SALT
- 1 1/2 CUPS HEAVY CREAM

Meringue:

1) Whisk egg whites until foamy. Add cream of tartar, salt and vanilla. Beat until thick.
2) Add granulated sugar, 1/4 cup at a time, beating for at least 30 seconds between each addition. Mixture should be satiny and hold a stiff peak.
3) Fit a large plain or star-shaped nozzle into a piping bag. Fill bag with meringue mixture (refill as needed).
4) Line a baking sheet with baking paper and pipe ten 3-inch diameter disks and ten 2-inch diameter disks, holding piping bag vertically, pulling bag upwards and forming a pointy turban shape.
5) Bake at 275°F for 90 minutes or until completely crisp. Set aside.

Filling:

1) Sprinkle gelatin over 1/4 cup passion fruit puree and set aside.
2) Combine remaining passion fruit puree and egg yolks.
3) Mix flour, sugar and salt in a small saucepan with a heavy bottom. Add passion fruit puree and egg yolk mixture. Stir constantly over low heat until mixture is thick and coats the back of the spoon. Set aside to cool.
4) Whip heavy cream until thick. Fold into the passion fruit mixture.

Assembling:

1) Place 2 tablespoons of passion fruit cream onto a 3-inch meringue disk. Place a 2-inch disk on top.
2) Place 1 tablespoons of passion fruit cream onto the 2-inch disk. Cover cream with raspberries.
3) Dab a little passion fruit cream on base of meringue "turban" and place on top of raspberries.
4) Repeat for all disks. Refrigerate pavlovas for 6-12 hours before serving.

Cocktail

The Feminine Mystique

1 oz Absolut Citron
1 oz Cointreau
1oz Chambord
Dash sugar
Splash fresh lemon juice

Combine ingredients, shake with ice and strain into a champagne glass. Top with champagne and garnish with brandy soaked cherries or a flower.

Music

•

Love to Love You Baby
Donna Summer/Polygram

•

Song in A Minor
Alicia Keys/J-Records

•

The Story of Bossa Nova
Blue Note

•

Je t'aime moi non plus
Serge Gainsbourg
Mercury/France

•

Fever
Peggy Lee/Prism

•

Memories, Chronicles and Declarations of Love
Marisa Monte/Blue Note

•

Music
Madonna/Warner Brothers

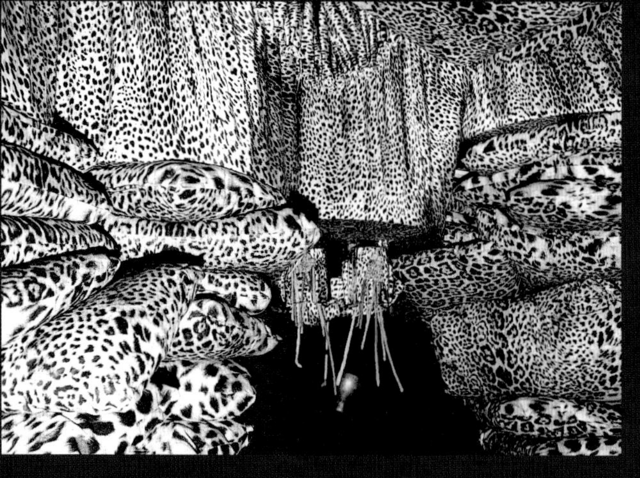

The Jungle

For a big party, few themes are as easy or exciting as this one. The African jungle holds a powerful allure for city folk, especially because it's the opposite of the cold, frenetic, overly civilized asphalt jungle in which we live. For the party pictured here, I made one simple request of my friends: to dress as wild things. And why not? Who doesn't love a few leopard spots or some face paint? What social circle doesn't include a rowdy man who's been quietly (or not so quietly) longing for an occasion to jump into a loincloth? But "Tarzan and Jane" is only one direction this party can take. Wild animals are another, especially if you're planning a kids' party, and African tribalism is a third, with its giant masks and body paint. For the hopelessly chic, safari—that clean, cool style made famous by Katharine Hepburn and revised in the seventies by Yves Saint Laurent—is another way to go. After all, for every loin cloth aspirant, there's a demure Isak Dinesen longing for a pair of khakis.

With the super-saturation of animal prints in stores, and the recent migration of tribal dance music into the mainstream, there's never been a better time than now to plan a jungle party. I hosted mine alongside Roberto Cavalli, the Italian designer so obsessed with animal prints that even his plane is upholstered in zebra stripes. Roberto has been experiencing a heyday in New York; women who would never have worn spots to a black-tie event, unless they were in their grandmothers' ratty ocelot coats, are suddenly doing so. Indeed, Roberto's wild romp proves that there's no better home for a party animal than in the jungle.

Entertainment

You might like to welcome your guests against a background of chirping birds, screeching monkeys and rustling leaves—jungle sounds you can easily find on an ambient CD. But for a dinner-dance, I prefer to get my friends in the mood right from the start with the sexy, persistent beat of tribal drums (buy a CD in the World Music section of any music store or hire actual drummers) that ease up only during dinner. Hiring parrot trainers also provides a cocktail-hour treat, and so do face painters to help

embellish people's costumes. Through Karin Bacon Events, we found a man with a giant canary-colored albino python, which greeted the guests as soon as they walked through the doors. I'll never forget Ivana Trump's face—she was utterly horrified at the sight of it, then relaxed and began to pet the snake's darting head. Before I knew it she was blowing it kisses and woman and beast were smiling for the camera like newlyweds!

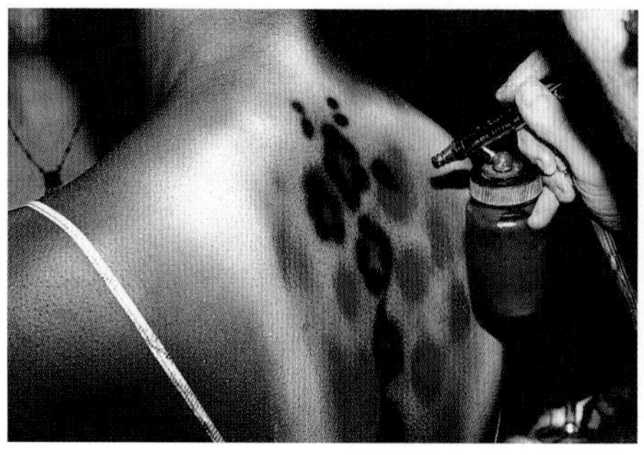

Dress

Animal prints, of course, raffia, tribal jewelry (teeth necklaces, Masai beading), *kenteh* cloth, African headdresses and African masks—or simply sexy safari clothing accessorized with snakeskin purses or alligator heels. The kind of cheap animal print fabric that can be purchased anywhere will make a terrific Fred Flintstone–style sarong, or a Wilma-worthy one-shoulder dress. But those are only the most obvious interpretations: Princess Olga of Greece had vines spilling out of her hair, Emma Askari tied a stuffed animal to her skirt and Celerie Kemble, in a ruffly white dress, was channeling a bird of paradise. The body painters we had on hand did much to embellish this theme—especially for those guests who had only a leopard scarf—but they weren't essential. With a jungle theme, it's easy to get people in the mood.

Invitations

The imagery associated with this theme makes invitations simple: leopard spots, zebra stripes, tribal regalia like masks, shields and raffia, dark wood, drums, yew trees, bamboo, wildflowers—or a photograph of Ava Gardner in *Mogambo* or Katharine Hepburn in *The African Queen*. I happen to love animal prints that are recolored on the computer in whimsical ways. For the Cavalli party, for example, we sent out silver invitation cards that flashed a faint background of blue zebra stripes. Most stationers will have zebra or leopard envelopes for these. Likewise, any inexpensive fabric shop will sell reams of leopard print: Cut out squares of the fabric, back it with cardboard, and paint the details in bright red or green. If you're throwing a jungle party for children—a theme they adore—pick up tiny stuffed lions or tigers, string small invitation cards to their necks and pop them in the mail. If you have the time and the money, send each person a boxed African mask (or an imitation of one). Or, buy some dark boxes or envelopes and fill them with rich green leaves along with the invitation.

Décor

Roberto Cavalli has great stores of leopard-print fabric at his disposal, and I can't begin to imagine how many yards he used for the party shown here—for seatbacks and tablecloths, napkins, pillows, wall hangings and even the waiters' aprons. If you have multiple tables (but probably no more than four or five), name each after a different animal and cover it with the appropriate print: Zebra, tiger, python, parrot, to name only a few. Rather than escort cards, consider stationing a face painter at a table near the entrance with a list of names that correspond to different animal-themed tables. He or she can then lightly paint the face of each guest to correspond to the appropriate table; imagine the spectacle of ten trumped-up elephants sitting next to ten flamingos! One wonderful way to illustrate this theme is to turn a wall or two of your party space into a big screen and project African jungle footage and savanna scenery onto it. For our party, Roberto had another idea: He made silk scarves in the prints corresponding to each table and stuck them in clear vinyl envelopes that became the escort cards. We loaded the room with thick, knotty potted trees and set the tables with vivid rose-printed plates and the bamboo-enshrined votives we found in Chinatown. As centerpieces, we bought twisted-looking branches and spray-painted them red. These look fantastic and last forever—don't throw them out! (Repaint them gold for Christmas and orange for Halloween.)

Venue

With the proper lighting and decoration, almost any site can be transformed for a jungle party. We rented a raw space and just about wrapped it in leopard. But for a summer party (and this is a terrific theme for summer, as it permits people to don the skimpiest of clothes), an outdoor tent works beautifully. If you're throwing this party for kids, no locale is more thrilling than the zoo.

Tarzan and Jane move over! Everyone's inner animal shines through tonight for this tribal-funky scene. Feathers, animal prints, and lots of skin bring out the wild side of jungle revelers for an untamed, unbridled and very lively evening.

SERVES 6

Menu

MAIN COURSE

Blue Lagoon Salad of Shrimp and Lobster with Three-Pepper Coulis

INGREDIENTS

THREE-PEPPER COULIS:
- 2 CUPS WHITE WINE
- 2 SHALLOTS, CHOPPED
- SALT AND FRESHLY GROUND PEPPER
- 1 CLOVE GARLIC, CRUSHED
- 1 GREEN PEPPER, DICED
- 1 RED PEPPER, DICED
- 1 YELLOW PEPPER, DICED

SALAD:
- 18 SLICES OF VINE-RIPENED TOMATOES, 1/8 OF AN INCH
- 16 LEAVES OF RED OAK LETTUCE, WASHED
- 12 OZ PAPAYA PEELED AND CHOPPED
- 36 SLICES SEEDLESS CUCUMBER, 1/8-INCH
- 3 2-LB LOBSTERS, BOILED, TAIL MEAT CUT INTO 24 SLICES AND CLAW MEAT REMOVED FROM SHELL
- 18 SHRIMP, PEELED, DEVEINED, BOILED AND BUTTERFLIED

PREPARATION

Three-Pepper Coulis

1) Combine the white wine, shallots, garlic, salt and pepper in a saucepan, cook over medium heat until sauce is reduced by one-third.

2) Divide reduction into 3 saucepans and add 1 kind of pepper to each pan. Simmer over low heat until peppers are tender. Remove from heat and allow to cool.

3) After cooling, pour the red pepper sauce into a blender and process at high speed for about 1 minute. Pass through a fine sieve, season with salt and pepper and set aside. Repeat the same process for the green and yellow peppers.

4) Cover and chill. Sauces may be kept refrigerated for several days.

Blue Lagoon Salad

1) On each of the 6 plates, place 3 tomato slices in a triangle shape. Place 1 oak lettuce leaf at 12 o'clock, scoop 2 ounces of papaya salsa into the center, and encircle with 6 slices of cucumber overlapping each other.

2) Arrange 4 slices of lobster tail side by side on each plate, placing the lobster claw in the center. On each tomato, place 1 shrimp, upright, with tail facing center and curving inwards.

3) Spoon the pepper coulis artfully over shellfish.

Cocktail

Sweet Ginger Brown

4 oz dark rum
1 tsp fresh ginger,
2 tbsp brown sugar
2 lemon wedges
3 lime wedges

Combine ingredients, shake with ice and pour into a cocktail glass. Garnish with fresh ginger.

Music

•

The Lion Sleeps Tonight
The Tokens/RCA
•

Jungle Love
Gladys Knight & The Pips
Columbia River
•

The Lion
Youssou N'dour/Virgin
•

Stranded in the Jungle
The Cadets/ACE/U.K.
•

Soul Makossa
Manu Dibango/Unidisc
•

Jungle Fever
Stevie Wonder /Motown
•

Mondo Afrika
Arc 21
•

Palo Conga
Sabu/Blue Note

Art

As its title suggests, the party shown here was a serious celebration of art—thrown by Eva Lorenzotti, an art maven, and Rachel Lehmann, whose New York gallery, Lehmann Maupin, is one of the nerve centers of the international contemporary art scene. Artists like Ross Bleckner, Casey Cook and Pedro Barbeito, along with a flurry of uptown art lovers, filed into the gallery for cocktails and dinner behind two candlelit gauze scrims; it was a spare and sophisticated affair, punctuated by a surprise musical performance piece. But despite what this chic version might suggest, art is a wonderfully versatile party theme.

While the party shown here had a built-in art world reserve about it, you might do a tongue-in-cheek artsy-fartsy soirée, where your black-turtlenecked guests circle the room and an old black-and-white Fellini film plays silently on the wall before a dinner of outrageously pretentious food. Or you can do a completely light-hearted finger painting party: Hang white rolls of paper over your walls and on the tables and invite people—very young, very old or both—to scribble away.

Dress

This theme party needn't enforce a dress code; we didn't with this one. But if you're throwing a painting party, ask your guests to wear their dirtiest jeans and T-shirts so that they can mess themselves up liberally with art supplies. Alternately, come as your favorite artist or, even more fun, your favorite art object. If your friends are an enterprising lot, you'll have men dressed in Dalí mustaches or with one ear in bandages, or as ominous Magritte heroes; you'll see lady Mona Lisas, Venuses and Virgin Marys, and, if there's a little girl in the room, perhaps a perfect Velázquez infanta. If there's a Duchamp fan among them, you may even get a nude descending a staircase!

Invitations

For their party, Eva and Rachel wanted an invitation with a spare, raw look—as though the card had been shaved straight from the tree trunk and delivered, still slick with paint, direct from the sculptor's studio. They sent their guests heavy decoupage invitations made from plywood rectangles; the details were collaged, then covered in intensely glossy polyurethane. But you can make richly illustrative invitations simply by splattering paint onto red, yellow or blue cards. Alternately, you can send mini-busts or paints and paintbrushes, or even a small canvas with the party details painted or stenciled on it. For a bit of fun, send each guest a pack of crayons or pastels and a five-by-seven-inch note card on which to do a quick self portrait; have your guests send you their portraits so you can mount a little art show on the day of the party.

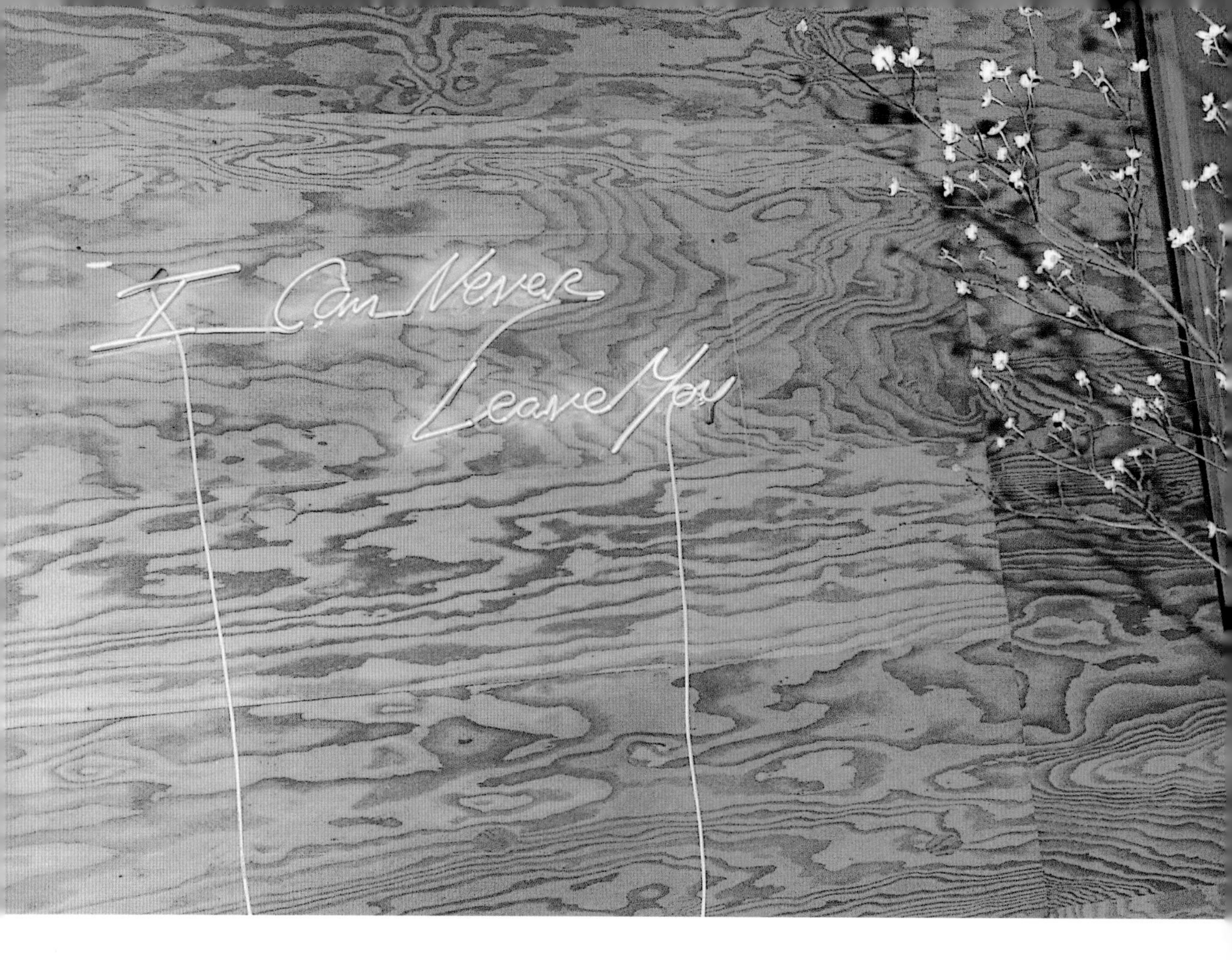

Décor

A beautiful work of art rarely looks better than when it's set off against a stark, white wall. The same goes for people—which is why the look I wanted for this party was sparse and uncluttered, very much a departure from the lushness I favor. In the central hall of the gallery, we set up two long dining tables that would also function as vitrines through which guests could view the art. (Imagine, for example, the illicit thrill of setting your plate down on Nefertiti's head!)

To do this, we laid cloths on simple plywood tables and placed drawings and photographs from the gallery on top of them. Then, we built up the tables on the sides with raw wooden blocks, and laid giant plexiglass plates over the blocks to create the actual dinner table, which, because it was clear, was also a window into the art on display. On top of the plexiglass, we set up still lifes for centerpieces, keeping the rest of the table simple—with clear votives and tall dogwood branches. Plexiglass trays full of votives hung from the ceiling.

For a lighter-hearted art party buy a few yards of white linen and some paint and make your own Jackson Pollock tablecloths. Set primary-colored ceramic plates, and use tall vases full of paintbrushes as centerpieces (which your guests could use during and after the meal). You might even monogram artists' smocks and lay them on chair backs.

Or, instead of turning your friends' self-portraits into a mini-gallery, lay them on the plates in lieu of place cards; everyone will enjoy running around deciphering the pictures. For more fun, have a few quirky and inexpensive materials on hand—lemons and tin foil, say—and invite your friends to create offbeat centerpieces. I assure you that even the disasters will look terrific.

Entertainment

People in New York can be deadly serious about their parties. Many of them forget that they're only parties, after all, and that parties are meant for pleasure. Instead, hosts of all kinds so often throw parties-as-performances, which you leave feeling either ravished by your host's skills, appalled by their showmanship or bored to tears by the heavy hand that makes so many of these parties seem like competitions. And even after all the dazzling efforts, you don't always feel you've had fun. The problem is that few people dare to go out on a limb to try something new and different; they'd much rather be correct and *comme il faut*. It's surprise, in one form or another, that's at the core of the very best parties. As a guest, you want an injection of your host's personality—and as a host, I hope you want to see your friends laughing, not simply saying "wow." It's very easy to go out and hire people to produce those wows, but it can come at the cost of flair. New Yorkers, especially, have such wide access to so many people's talents; so combine a tin of caviar with the guy you found sketching or singing in Central Park! That's what we did for this party: Quite simply, we went out and found a few singers we liked in the street; in the context of a chic gallery dinner, they were perfect.

This party is the ultimate blending of uptown sophistication and downtown cool. Like the contrast between the spare white walls of a gallery and the colorful variety of the art that hangs there, there's harmony in contrasts. But whether cerebral or funky, classy or hip, the key concept here is to just let your creativity run wild.

Menu

SERVES 4

MAIN COURSE

INGREDIENTS

PREPARATION

Potato Galette with Smoked Salmon

- 1 IDAHO POTATO
- 1 BUNCH PARSLEY, LEAVES ONLY, CHOPPED
- 1 BUNCH CHIVES, CHOPPED
- CORN OIL
- 2 TBSP BUTTER
- 8 THIN SLICES SMOKED SALMON
- CRÈME FRAÎCHE
- 1 OZ SALMON ROE

1) Thinly julienne one Idaho potato on a mandoline. Wash well to remove starch and squeeze between paper towels to remove excess moisture. Season lightly with salt, pepper, parsley and chopped chives. Let sit for 30 minutes.
2) Cover bottom of 7-inch nonstick skillet with corn oil and place over medium-high heat. When lightly smoking, add 1 tablespoon butter.
3) Add potato slices to skillet. Stir with wooden spoon to coat well with corn oil. Smooth potato to cover bottom of pan, lower heat slightly.
4) Cut remaining tablespoon of butter into pieces and place around galette to melt. When bottom is golden brown, flip and repeat on other side.
5) Remove and drain on paper towels. Arrange thin slices of smoked salmon around the galette.
6) In the center, place a large dollop of crème fraîche. Spoon salmon roe on top of crème fraîche. Sprinkle with chives.

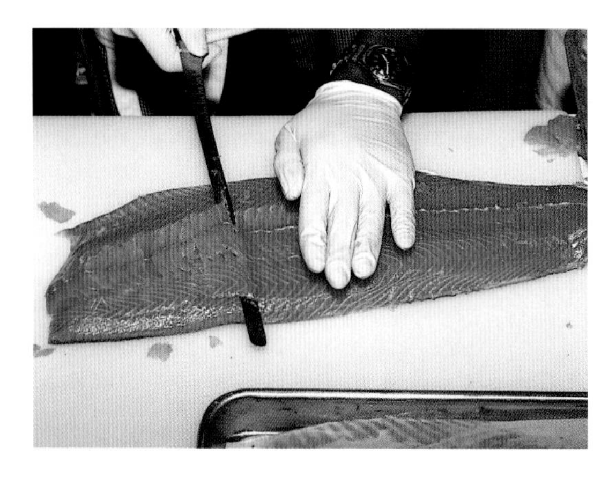

Herb-Crusted Rack of Lamb

- 2 CLOVES GARLIC, PEELED AND MINCED
- 2 TBSP OLIVE OIL
- 2 SPRIGS ROSEMARY, LEAVES ONLY
- 1 CUP UNSEASONED BREAD CRUMBS
- 1/4 CUP PARSLEY, LEAVES ONLY, CHOPPED
- 1 TSP *EACH* SALT AND FRESHLY GROUND BLACK PEPPER
- 1 LAMB RACK, ROAST READY, FRENCHED (ASK YOUR BUTCH ER TO PREPARE THIS FOR YOU)
- DIJON MUSTARD

1) Preheat oven to 350°F. In a mixing bowl combine the garlic, olive oil and rosemary.
2) In a bowl, combine the bread crumbs, parsley and 1/2 teaspoon *each* salt and pepper. Set aside.
3) Place prepared lamb fat side down on a baking sheet. Rub the bone side with garlic mixture, season with remaining salt and pepper. Place in preheated oven and bake for 20 minutes.
4) Remove from oven. Turn lamb over and let sit for 10 minutes.
5) With a kitchen brush, spread Dijon mustard over the fat side of lamb.
6) Press the bread crumb mixture into the mustard. Place back on the baking sheet, crumb side up. Return to the the oven for 10 more minutes or a little longer depending on how well you would like it cooked.
7) Remove from oven, let sit a few minutes. Slice between the bones, 3 bones to a portion.

Cocktail

Strawberry Mojito

4 oz Captain Morgan's Spiced Rum
Freshly muddled strawberries
Mint
Brown sugar

Combine ingredients, shake with ice and serve in a cocktail glass garnished with a strawberry.

Music

•

Café Blue
Patricia Barber/Blue Note
•

Blue Train
John Coltrane/Blue Note
•

My Life in the Bush of Ghosts
Brian Eno/Warner Brothers
•

Fascinoma
Jon Hassell/Water Lily
•

Shostakovich String Quartets
Polygram
•

Kind of Blue
Miles Davis/Sony
•

Kafka Fragments
György Kurtág/Ondine
•

Good Evening Vietnam

Countess Muriel Brandolini, the New York decorator and hostess, is half Vietnamese and spent the first twelve years of her life in Vietnam. Few people think Muriel looks Vietnamese at all, but, as she likes to say, "It's all in the mind." That's the attitude that Muriel likes to give to her dinner parties, which are very often small, twinkling Asian affairs. Muriel always entertains at home, in the bamboo-lined garden of her Upper East Side townhouse or in the dining room decorated with Boulle chairs and a Swedish dining table, as well as a lavish Chinese opium bed on which her guests like to recline after dinner, cigarette in one hand and drink in the other.

Like most people with great taste, Muriel is also very opinionated. The following are her thoughts on throwing the perfect intimate dinner party with a Vietnamese theme.

Invitations

For a dinner at home, I find invitation cards too formal. The hostess should invite everyone by phone followed a reminder in the mail. Never have a secretary do the calling—it's insulting not to be invited by the actual host of a party. If I were to do a giant Vietnamese dinner outside the house, I'd do it a little differently. I'd send invitation cards with Vietnamese imagery on them—like a girl with long black hair on a bicycle, wearing typical Vietnamese garb and a cap. For place cards, I'd use Vietnamese straw hats that people could take home.

Dress

The dress code is simple: wide-legged, silky pants with a long, robe-like top that's slit and buttoned on the side. (Or, if you prefer, beautiful Asian-silk dresses . . .)

Décor

My dining room is very Asian-looking to begin with. It's just a cozy little room, with rose-colored Indian fabric on the walls, 17th-century settees and 18th-century Japanese blinds. For the dinner shown here, I used a Vietnamese tablecloth hand-embroidered with pink blossoms. On top of that I laid china decorated with pink peonies and rimmed with gold. I put fresh peonies on the table, too, because I feel they always make a party look Asian. On top of the China I set wooden bowls and ebonized chopsticks, which provide a nice contrast to the European porcelain.

Menu

In Asia, each meal is a ceremony in itself. The Vietnamese always serve about ten dishes, the idea being to eat tiny portions of many different things. It's a novel and exciting way of eating. But with little portions, the food has to be especially wonderful, with every plate memorable in its own way.

And despite what you might think from Vietnamese restaurants in America, in Vietnam people don't really eat dessert. I like to follow this rule, so I serve only savories followed by, at most, a simple lemon tart.

As a hostess, it's your job to be sure that the drink is constantly—and I mean constantly—being poured. The more your guests are flushed and high, the more they'll want to keep the party going.

Venue

A dinner party is, very simply, the selection of guests—that's more important than any other component. Of course you must establish the right ambience—with the way you present the table and the food and the way you make up the room—but more than anything ambience is created by the people you invite.

As for the guests, I don't like stuffy or pompous people. I like fun folks who love to eat. The last thing I want is a person who's going to munch on a lettuce leaf, and I'm no keener on a person who only wants to make small talk. We have to do enough of that outside our houses. The home is for good friends only.

That genial triad of good friends, warm atmosphere and fabulous food is perhaps the most sublime combination of all. Now add an exotic, luxurious and absolutely beautiful setting and you've got a party people will talk about for a long time to come.

SERVES 4

Menu

APPETIZER

Vietnamese Spring Rolls

INGREDIENTS

- 3/4 CUP OF TREE EAR MUSHROOMS
- SMALL BAG (2 OZ OR LESS) OF MUNG-BEAN OR CELLOPHANE NOODLE VERMICELLI
- 1 LB GROUND PORK
- 1 LB SHRIMP, SHELLED, DEVEINED AND MINCED
- 12 FRESH WATER CHESTNUTS (OR 1 CUP OF JICAMA), DICED
- 1 CUP DICED VIDALIA ONIONS
- 1 SMALL FRESH CARROT, GRATED
- 1 TBSP SUGAR
- 1 TBSP FISH SAUCE, AND SAUCE FOR DIPPING (NUOC MAM)
- 3 CLEAN KITCHEN TOWELS
- 1 PACKAGE ROSE BRAND RICE PAPER
- 2 QTS CORN OIL
- LETTUCE, MINT, CILANTRO AND BASIL LEAVES, WASHED AND DRIED

PREPARATION

1) Soak mushrooms in warm water for 30 minutes. Wash and rinse several times until the water is clear. Remove hard stems and chop into small pieces.

2) Soak vermicelli in warm water for 20 minutes, drain and cut with scissors into 2-inch lengths.

3) To make filling, mix pork, shrimp, water chestnuts, onion, carrot, sugar and fish sauce in a large bowl.

4) To make spring rolls, fill a large bowl with warm water. Lay one towel on flat surface. One at a time, dip four sheets of rice paper into warm water and lay flat on towel. Cover with second towel, and repeat. Then cover the pile with the third towel. Turn the pile upside down. Remove the top towel.

5) One by one, assemble the spring rolls, as follows: Carefully peel a sheet of rice paper from the towel, lay it flat on the counter. Use about 2/3 tablespoon of filling for each roll, shaped into a cylinder about 1-inches long and 1-inch in diameter, placed on the paper one inch from the edge. Fold the sides up, then roll paper.

6) To cook the spring rolls, use a deep-fryer, preferably electric for temperature control. Put oil in fryer and heat to 350°F. Place rolls in basket and deep fry until golden brown. Remove and drain on paper.

7) Rolls should be wrapped in a lettuce leaf along with mint, cilantro or basil leaves, and dipped in extra fish sauce.

Since this recipe is time-consuming, you may want to prepare a day ahead of time, deep frying halfway to cook, but not browning. Keep in the refrigerator, and deep fry to golden brown just before serving.

Cocktail

Singapore Sling

4 oz gin
Orange juice and fresh lemon (equal parts)
Dash of sugar

Combine ingredients, shake and serve over ice in a cocktail glass with a Benedictine float. Garnish with fresh fruit.

Music

•

Buddha-Bar (vols. 1-4)
George V
•

Lullaby for the Moon
Japanese Music for Koto
Shakuka chi
Blue Note
•

Asia Classics (vols. 1 & 2)
Luaka Bop
•

Ultra Lounge, Vol. 1
Mondo Exotica/Capitol
•

Kiss of the Dragon
Soundtrack/Virgin
•

Dragon Red & Cherry Blossom

At the start of spring, just as the long colonnades of white-blossomed cherry trees began to explode in the parks of New York, my friend Bettina Zilkha threw a sumptuous Chinese dinner-dance at Doubles, the private club in the Sherry Netherland hotel. As a theme for a party, China—and Asia in general—promises the kind of sophisticated, heavily made-up glamour that people love to put on for a night.

What's more, nearly everyone has something Chinese in her wardrobe: a cheongsam, perhaps, or even just a jacket with silken embroidery and frog closures. This makes the party perfect for a big group. (High buns, white powder, jade or onyx jewelry and rice-paper parasols are easy enough to add.) Thanks to Hollywood, especially—think Rita Hayworth in *The Lady from Shanghai*—those touchstones of elegant, old-world Pekingese social life have a tantalizing hold on the American imagination. And so does Chinese food!

Décor

Doubles—a rather buttoned-up subterranean salon that caters unabashedly to the city's ladies who lunch—isn't the first place I'd think of to put on a big Chinese dinner-dance for 180 people. But the party shown here demonstrates how dramatically the character of a place can be transformed with only the subtlest alterations. Bettina's only requirement was that the venue be red, and Doubles has deep red walls and tall red damask banquettes to recommend it. Beyond that, our task was simple. We lit some jasmine incense to set the mood and let the flowers do the rest. David Beahm filled the place with tall pink and white cherry blossoms, weaving in crab apple branches to give fullness to his arrangements.

The blossoms stretched up to form a grand canopy over the dance floor, and, lit dramatically from below with tiny bright bulbs, they cast wild, flickering shadows on the ceiling. The WASP frippery of Doubles was further undercut by the dozens of paper dragons hanging in the bathrooms, and by the giant red pillar candles perched on every imaginable surface. Rice paper globe lanterns, occasionally lit with red (instead of white) bulbs, replaced traditional lighting. Because of the lavishness of the space (to say nothing of the costumes!), we opted for a simple table, laid in red and fuchsia Dupione silk with heaps of hot-pink glass votives, white plates and Chinese paper-wrapped chocolates with fortunes inside. But you might use Chinese fans as placemats, or in miniature, as place cards. As centerpieces, we used polished cast aluminum squares heaped with polished river stones that supported poppies, anemones and gloriosa lilies.

Behind each place card, joss—the traditional Chinese "spirit money"—rested on a pink damask napkin. On the bar, red candles floated in bowls along with fragrant gardenias. We served from red lacquer trays and used porcelain plates, but wooden lacquer plates would work beautifully, and inexpensively, if you pay a visit to your local Chinatown. (Often, Chinatown stores will be willing to rent you their wares for 10 percent of the retail price.) If you have as many tables as Bettina did, you should name each one after a traditional Chinese virtue: Peace, prosperity, wisdom, luck, serenity, truth, fulfillment, bliss, love, knowledge, courage, intuition, wit, faith. As escort cards, fill fortune cookies with paper slips indicating the table name (Chinatown bakeries can do this), wrap them in cellophane and tie name tags on with pink and white ribbons. And as souvenirs, if you're feeling lavish, place a pink or red T-shirt bearing the name of the guest written in Chinese characters at each seat. For entertainment, we hired Chinese musicians who played traditional instruments.

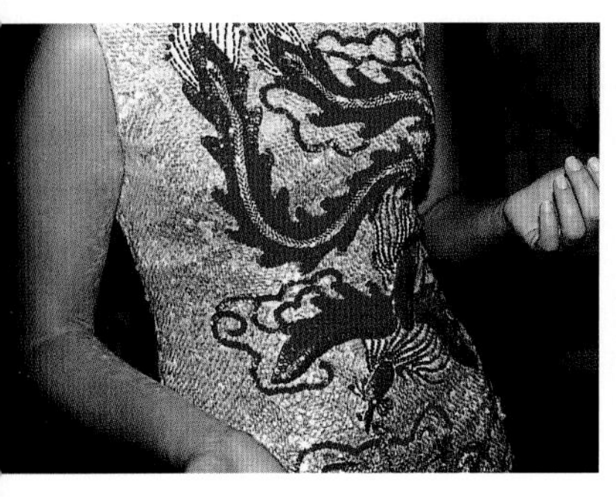

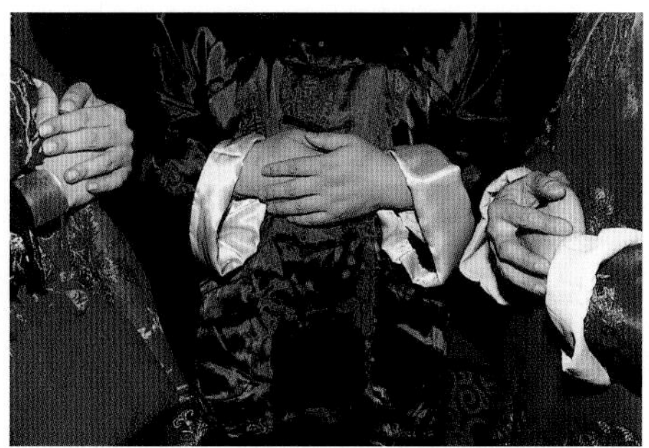

Dress

Like all the most effective themes, this one allowed for varied, but always elaborate, interpretations. Women put on everything from chunky turquoise beads to pearls; they wore elaborate earrings and chopsticks in their hair, or black bobbed wigs and Chinese silken tasseled caps. That season, Christian Dior had made kitschy Chinese embroidered T-shirts and skirts that a handful of women wore for the occasion—but kimonos and $20 Chinese pajamas work fine. The men—when they didn't simply wear crisp red or pink shirts—raced to Chinatown instead of Shanghai Tang in search of inexpensive mandarin robes and jackets in red and black silk, which they wore with black pants and slippers. Hamish Bowles, of course, wore a bespoke pink velvet suit, and Alex Papachristidis was almost impossible to recognize in the long black mustache that was the punch line to his ancient Chinese emperor costume.

Invitations

The symbolism attached to this theme is obvious enough: Twisting dragons, lacquer screens, lanterns, pagodas, parasols, fans and chopsticks. Many of the Chinese packaged goods you can buy at Asian markets morph into excellent invitations: Send collapsible paper lanterns on whose sides you've painted the party details, for example; or send fortune cookies with the invitations tucked inside. Buy inexpensive red or black lacquer chopsticks and bind them with a strip of shiny pink wrapping paper on which you've written the party details in black or gold ink. Bettina kept it simple, opting for a pink card embellished with Chinese characters. (The envelopes can be sealed with a wax Chinese character.) Keep in mind that customizing the writing always costs more; what Bettina discovered was that Judith Ness, who produced her invitations, had made up some Chinese text for another client a few years earlier. We went ahead and printed that very text on Bettina's cards, hoping no one would realize that the square, calligraphic image at the top actually said "Michelle and Michael." Of course, no one did!

The other side of the world becomes an exotic place where the senses are awakened and good fortune is cultivated in all one does. Luscious silks, deep reds and golds, rarified flavor and mysterious music envelop guests who revel in this otherworldly atmosphere.

Menu

SERVES 4

MAIN COURSE

Crispy Seared Salmon with Sesame Spinach

INGREDIENTS

SALMON MARINADE:

- A LEMONGRASS BRANCH, CUT FINELY
- 2 TSP GRATED GINGER
- 1 TSP CHOPPED GARLIC
- 2 TSP CILANTRO LEAVES, CHOPPED
- 2 TSP PARSLEY LEAVES, CHOPPED
- 2 TSP FRESH LEMON JUICE
- 1 CUP CANOLA OIL

SALMON:

- 4 6-OZ SALMON FILETS WITH THE SKIN ON
- 1 TSP OLIVE OIL
- SALT AND FRESHLY GROUND BLACK PEPPER

SESAME STEAMED SPINACH:

- 2 TSP SESAME SEEDS
- 1 TSP CANOLA OIL
- 1 TSP CHOPPED GARLIC
- 1 TSP RICE WITH VINEGAR
- 2 TSP SOY SAUCE
- 1 TSP LEMON JUICE
- 1 LB SPINACH LEAVES, CLEANED AND STEMMED

PREPARATION

Crispy Seared Salmon

1) In a glass dish, combine all the marinade ingredients, mix well.
2) Place your salmon on top of the marinade, skin side up. (Use a small enough dish that the marinade covers the salmon but not the skin, or the skin will not get crispy when cooking.) Refrigerate for 1 hour.
3) Place heavy skillet over high heat. When very hot, add olive oil. Immediately place salmon in skillet,skin side down. Lightly salt and pepper the filet.
4) Let the salmon cook almost all the way through on the skin side only, about 6 minutes for rare. You can actually see the salmon as it cooks The skin side should be very crispy and the meat side slightly undercooked and juicy. (If you prefer your fish well done, you may flip it onto its meat side and cook for another 2 minutes or so.)

Sesame Steamed Spinach

1) Place a saucepan over medium heat. Add sesame seeds and toast lightly. Set aside. In same saucepan, heat canola oil. Add garlic and sauté until lightly browned.
2) Pour in rice wine vinegar. Add soy sauce and lemon juice. Let simmer and reduce by half.
3) Place spinach leaves in the pan and stir until they begin to wilt, about 1 minute, cook about 1 minute more.
4) Remove the pan from the heat and drain the liquid. Sprinkle toasted sesame seeds over spinach.

To serve, divide the spinach evenly onto 4 plates, place a salmon fillet on top of each.

Cocktail

Cherry Blossom Caipirinha

4 oz Cachaca
2 tbs sugar
Freshly muddled cherries
Lime wedges

Combine ingredients, shake with ice and serve in a cocktail glass. Top with club soda. Garnish with edible flowers.

Dragon Rd Dark Forest

1 oz Stoli Razberi Vodka
1 oz Stoli Vanil Vodka
Freshly muddled black raspberries
Raspberry puree
Cranberry juice

Combine ingredients, shake with ice and serve in a chilled martini glass. Garnish with fresh berries.

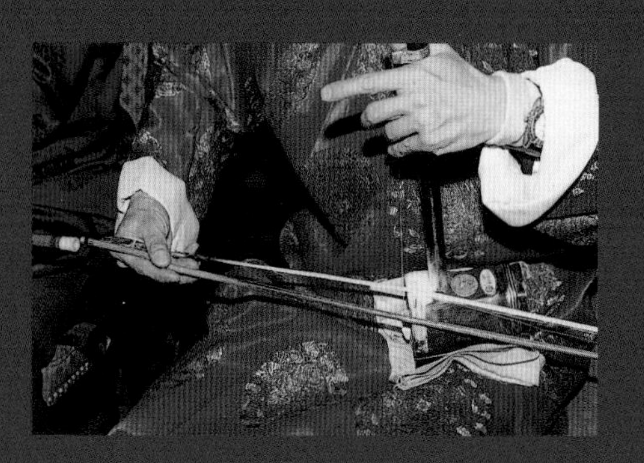

Music

•

Asia Classics · (vols. 1 & 2)
Luaka Bop
•

Koto Music of Japan
Zumi-Kai/Legacy
•

Crouching Tiger, Hidden Dragon
(Soundtrack)/Sony
•

Madama Butterfly
Maria Callas/EMI Classics
•

Silk Road Journeys
Yo Yo Ma/Sony
•

Golden Toga

Adding the color gold to this hackneyed collegiate theme is a perfect way to make it glamorous and grown-up. Gold also allows for a little flexibility for those who are too shy to trot out a toga, or who find themselves unable to summon inspiration out of the requisite plain white sheet. This theme also makes for a louche, sexy party, one where your guests will feel as comfortable sprawled out on the carpet as they will undulating on the dance floor. Although classical Greece is the obvious touchstone here, I prefer to think of the decadence of imperial Rome, whose debauched rulers were voluptuaries ruled by their thirst for pleasure. For ideas, Hollywood will help you: There's the palace atmosphere of *Spartacus*, of course, and Tinto Brass's infamous *Caligula*, a horrible movie that, for all its sexual explicitness, paints as rich a picture of the orgiastic Roman court as you could ever wish for.

This theme works best for a more casual event—one in which your guests know each other well enough that they'll feel comfortable embracing the theme and the roles that accompany it. Keep in mind that it's an almost regressive theme, in which the gender roles follow pretty strict lines (not that it isn't always fun to cross them!): The men are powerful—I was thrilled to see how many gladiator costumes turned up at our party—and the women, in marvelously sexy Grecian peplums, look as though they're present solely for the purpose of satisfying men's appetites. For this party, I anointed a quorum of male hosts I knew would love those roles: Prince Pavlos of Greece, Vikram Chatwal, Todd Meister, Lapo Elkann and Alexandre von Furstenberg. We threw the party at Alex's mother's West Village studio, turning it into the site of an opulent bacchanal—where none of the sophomoric stink of *Animal House* penetrated the air.

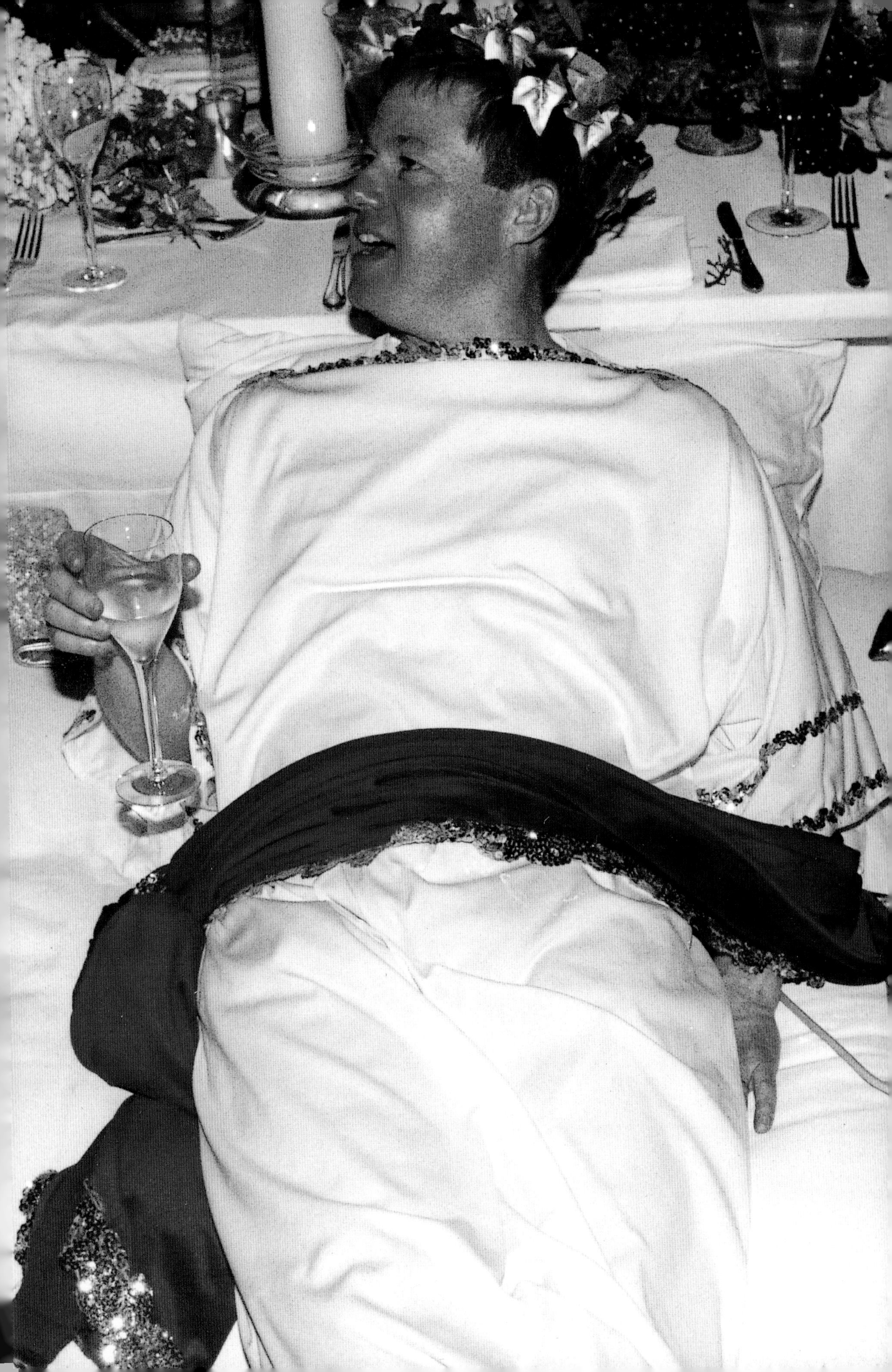

Entertainment

Ancient Roman parties were peopled with jugglers, lute players, singers and magicians who wove their way through the crowd—and this works well here. For my party, we hired female models who wandered around feeding guests grapes from golden trays until our hosts sounded the dinner bell—which in this case was a big brass gong.

During dinner, toga-clad drummers heightened the atmosphere, keeping time to the rhythms already being offered by the deejay. It might also be nice to have a face painter on hand to transform your guests into the busts of gods and goddess on gold coins. And in lieu of a crystal ball reader, you can hire a soothsayer to read fortunes from scattered leaves.

Décor

This is a party whose success really hangs upon creating a dining room fit for the gods (I'm thinking of Dionysus, of course, not Apollo!). With the help of Bardin Palomo, the New York event planners, we erected several 24-foot-long low tables, draped them with white cloths and laid out long, dramatic centerpieces comprised of spiky branches of white coral, white plaster busts, three-foot-tall Ionic columns, gold and verdigris compotes filled with cascading fruit and foliage, white flowers in antique-looking frosted glass urns and glowing candles inside clear glass hurricanes. Then, to complement my guests' costumes, we placed a laurel wreath at each setting.

Underneath the tables, we unrolled long strips of white carpeting, which we topped with 150 assorted pillows: white, gold lamé and gold-and-white striped. We projected giant images of laurel wreaths onto three walls, tacked billowing white fabric to the ceiling, and placed eight-foot columns wrapped in fresh green garlands throughout the suite of rooms. In the cocktail area, we suspended sheer floor-to-ceiling curtains though which guests seemed to flow and disappear. Dramatic large-scale antique containers filled with fragrant orange branches studded the corners, and pillar candles, votives and glowing torchères provided the dim, warm light.

To keep your décor simple, build a long table out of cinderblocks and a plywood plank, and cover it with white cotton cloth. The gold lamé cushions are a terrific touch, and because this fabric is very inexpensive it's worth having a few pillowcases made. Your table will look terrific simply dressed in ivy and grapes. If you can find an inexpensive plaster (or plastic) bust or two, it will make the perfect whimsical centerpiece. Add touches of gold by substituting gold votives for white, and spray-painting some of the ivy or dusting the tables with gold glitter—as long as you don't mind the mess the next day. Feathers are another fun addition to this theme; arrangements of white and gold-sprayed feathers will be a refreshing—and much less expensive—substitute for flowers.

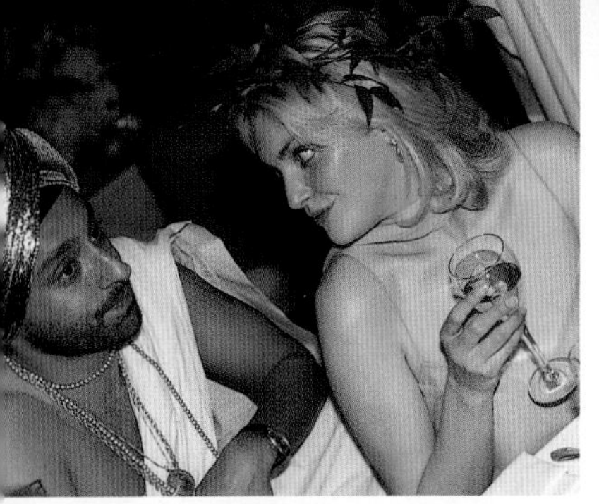

Invitations

As I've said before, depending on how daring your friends are, the toughest part of throwing a theme party can be getting guests to dress the part. A little nudge from the invitation goes very far—which is why, for this party, we sent each of my guests a standard-issue black paper shopping bag which contained a white toga-ready sheet cinched with gold cord.

When the time came, some guests used only these two elements; others used them and embellished them according to their fancy; but most people found something altogether more fabulous. we also enclosed a card emblazoned with the image, repeated five times, of a Roman statue. The base of each image bore the spray-painted initials of each host—an irreverent, modernizing touch, as if they'd gone to the Louvre and vandalized the statuary! This card was very easy to make: We plucked images straight from Internet to create a simple but evocative invitation that can be sent with or without a toga or other accessories.

For a more lavish invitation, consider sending golden medallions with the details embossed on them, or laurel wreaths tagged with the party details. Here are key symbols to keep in mind: grapes, olives and laurel, crumbling marble, Zeus's thunderbolt and Artemis's bow and arrow, the mosaic floors and frescos of Pompei, grapes, Greek amphorae, Roman busts and Medusa's snaky head.

Dress

Our guests were incredibly creative, cutting and gilding their white sheets, crafting togas out of silver-sequined disco fabric and draping themselves in golden saris and Balinese sarongs. Our more fashion-conscious friends picked up Grecian goddess dresses, or dusted off their old Mary McFadden Fortuny-silk peplums. Women wore gold headbands, diadems and gilded wreaths, lots of gold snaky jewelry and gold sandals. As for the men, those who forsook their togas chose gladiator gear instead—complete with chest plates and shields. Harry Lefrak just couldn't bring himself to wear either, so as a compromise he wore his toga on top of a dark suit. For my part, I went as Cleopatra (a famous Roman's lover, so it does count!), while my friend Alex Kramer cobbled together what may have been the night's most inspired costume: She somehow managed to make a beautiful Grecian dress out of a white curtain she bought at Bed, Bath & Beyond.

Venue

A large, raw, white space works perfectly for this theme since you'll want to confine your color palette to white, green, purple and gold. If you're renting a restaurant or part of one, keep this in mind, and stick with a Greek or Italian eatery according to your vision. While this party is lush, it's not necessarily cozy, so look for a venue with high ceilings and a good deal of space.

Gods and goddesses, Roman emperors and concubines, maybe even a Cleopatra or two—everyone gets a chance to walk among the gods on the dizzy heights of champagne-drenched Olympus where the theme for the night is Dionysian bacchanal!

Menu

This theme invites either a Greek or a Roman menu, and we went for Greek. If yours is a late-night crowd, consider serving pasta for "breakfast" at around two in the morning. (This is standard practice at grand European parties.)

Taittinger, which sponsored this party, purveyed rivers of bubbling, golden champagne—the perfect drink for a gold-themed event. Here's a champagne cocktail you might try instead of serving the straight stuff.

SERVES 4

MAIN COURSE

Herb-Crusted Leg of Lamb

INGREDIENTS

- 1 4-5 LB LEG OF LAMB
- 1/4 CUP OLIVE OIL
- 1 TBSP GARLIC
- 1 BUNCH ITALIAN PARSLEY, LEAVES ONLY, CHOPPED
- 1 BUNCH THYME LEAVES ONLY, CHOPPED
- 1 BUNCH ROSEMARY, LEAVES ONLY, CHOPPED
- 1 TBSP CUMIN, FRESHLY GROUND
- 1 TBSP BLACK PEPPER, FRESHLY GROUND
- 2 TBSP KOSHER SALT
- BUTCHER'S TWINE

PREPARATION

1) Preheat over to 400°F. Butterfly leg of lamb, carefully removing tendons, gristle and fat without disturbing major muscle joints.
2) Sauté garlic lightly in olive oil. Add parsley, thyme and rosemary and sauté briefly, 1-2 minutes.
3) Heat cumin separately in small dry saute pan until fragrant. Add to herb mixture, along with pepper and salt.
4) Rub the interior of the leg with 1/3 of the spice mix and reassemble, tying firmly with the twine at 1-inch intervals.
5) Sear on 4 sides on a hot grill and place in preheated oven for 25 minutes. Rub remainder of herb and spice mixture on outside and finish with an additional 25 minutes in the oven.
6) Let the lamb rest 15 minutes before serving.

Cocktail

Classic Champagne Cocktail

In a champagne glass
pour champagne
over a brandy-soaked
sugar cube.
Garnish with
a twist of lemon.

Music

•

Saturday Night Fever
Soundtrack/Polygram
•

Boogie Nights
Soundtrack/Capitol
•

The Best of the Commodores
Polygram
•

You Can Dance
Madonna/Warner Brothers
•

Jump Back:
The Best of the Rolling Stones
(1971-1993)
EMI International
•

No More Drama
Mary J. Blige/MCA
•

Gold: Greatest Hits
Abba/Polygram
•

SOURCES:

HOT HACIENDA:
Caterer: Restaurant Associates
Décor: Ron Wendt Design
212.290.2428
Mariachi Band: Mariachi Bustamante 212.781.7123
Invitation Featured: Couturier de Cardboard Inc. 212.243.2225

THEATRICAL HEADS:
Caterer: Robbins Wolfe Eventeurs
www.robbinswolfe.com
New York, 212.924.6500
Décor: Tansy Design Associates
Invitation featured: Ellen Weldon Design 212.925.4483

1001 NIGHTS:
Décor: Color of Magic
212.967.5439
Contacts: Christine Ellis
Catherine & Ron Guilaldo
Caterer: Robbins Wolfe Eventeurs 212.924.6500
www.robbinswolfe.com
DJ: Topspin Entertainment
212.595.4499
Percussionists: Rogue Percussion Ensemble
Contact: Ron Guerrero
Belly Dancer: Amira Mor International Entertainment Co.
www.amiramor.com
Invitation featured: Ellen Weldon Design 212.925.4483

SKYSCRAPER GARDEN LUNCHEON:
Décor: David Beahm Design
212.279.1344
Caterer/location: Hotel Giraffe
212.685.7700
www.hotelgiraffe.com

SOUTHAMPTION LUAU:
Caterer/Location: Club Colette, Southampton
Décor: Anthony Todd Inc.
212.367.7363
Orchid leis from Hawaii:
www.sendleis.com
Invitations: Windigo
973.425.7681
DJ: Tony Kerr 631.287.1942
Steel Band: Vivian and the Merry Makers

BLACK AND WHITE:
Caterer: Taste 212.255.8571
Décor: EventQuest, Inc.
www.eventquest.com
212.966.3146
DJ: Tom Finn, Topspin Entertainment 212.595.4499
Invitation: Ellen Weldon Design
212.925.4483
Lighting Production: Finelite Productions, Inc. 609.978.1330

PRETTY IN PINK:
Invitation: BK Design
617.426.8255
www.BKinvitesU.com

SIGNATURE STYLES:
Photo boxes: JAM Paper
www.jampaper.com 800.8010.jam
Floral Arrangement and Design: Olivier Guigni of L'Olivier Floral Atelier 212.774.7676
Leather-bound library books: Argossy 212.753.4455
Magnifying glass: Authentic Models, Nostalgia from Bygone Days 800.888.1992
www.authenticmodels.com
Professional handwriting analysis by Graphology Consulting Group
Sheila Kurtz
Karan Charatan, lettering artist, or, Pro-Print
Wine: Terlato Imports
800.950.7676
Armani Casa Logo Candles from Armani Casa 212.334.1271

DRAGON RED AND CHERRY BLOSSOM PINK:
Caterer and Location:
Doubles Club 212.751.9595
Décor: David Beahm Design
212.279.1344
DJ: Tom Finn, Topspin Entertainment 212.595.4499
Invitations and escort fortune cookies: Judith Ness
212.348.5863
Invitation (fan featured):
Couturier de Cardboard, Inc.
212.243.2225
Chinese Musicians: Zhao Gang
212.722.4515

THE JUNGLE:
Producers of themed entertainment: Karin Bacon Events
212.307.9641
Caterer: Sterling Affair
212.686.4075
Venue: Bloom Ballroom
African Band: Ndombasi
201.963.6610
DJ: David Chang 212.501.8919

ART PARTY:
Décor: Bronson van Wyck
212.675.8601
Lighting Design: Litz Design StudioCaterer: Swifty's/RSVP Catering
Entertainment: Capella Spank

VIETNAMESE DINNER:
Chef: Minh Chau Gallagher
minchau@nyc.rr.com

SCENT OF A WOMAN:
Décor: Bardin Palomo Ltd.
Event Design and Production
212.989.6113
Invitation: Ellen Weldon Design
212.925.4483
Caterer: Serena Bass Inc. Events and Catering,
www.serenabass.com
Latin Dancers: Tony Meredith & Melanie Lapatin, Dance Times Square 212.994.9500
www.dancetimessquare.com

GOLDEN TOGA:
Décor: Bardin Palomo Ltd.
Event Design and Production
212.989.6113
Location: Diane von Furstenberg Theater
212.741.6607
Invitation: Sharp Communications, Inc. 212.829.0002
info@sharpthink.com
Caterer: Tentation, Potel & Chabot
info@tentation.net
DJ: David Chang 212.501.8919